SPSS
Regression Models™ 9.0

For more information about SPSS® software products, please visit our WWW site at *http://www.spss.com* or contact

Marketing Department
SPSS Inc.
233 South Wacker Drive, 11th Floor
Chicago, IL 60606-6307
Tel: (312) 651-3000
Fax: (312) 651-3668

SPSS Regression Models™ 9.0
Copyright © 1999 by SPSS Inc.
All rights reserved.
Printed in the United States of America.

2 3 4 5 6 7 8 9 0   04 03 02 01 00 99

ISBN 0-13-020404-8

Preface

SPSS® 9.0 is a powerful software package for microcomputer data management and analysis. The Regression Models option is an add-on enhancement that provides additional statistical analysis techniques. The procedures in Regression Models must be used with the SPSS 9.0 Base and are completely integrated into that system.

The Regression Models option includes procedures for:

- Weighted and two-stage least-squares regression
- Logistic regression
- Multinomial regression
- Nonlinear regression

The procedure for reliability analysis, formerly included in the Regression Models option, is now included in the Base.

Installation

To install Regression Models, follow the instructions for adding and removing features in the installation instructions supplied with the SPSS Base. (To start, double-click on the SPSS Setup icon.)

Compatibility

The SPSS system is designed to operate on many computer systems. See the materials that came with your system for specific information on minimum and recommended requirements.

Serial Numbers

Your serial number is your identification number with SPSS Inc. You will need this serial number when you call SPSS Inc. for information regarding support, payment, or an upgraded system. The serial number was provided with your Base system. Before using the system, please copy this number to the registration card.

Registration Card

Don't put it off: *fill out and send us your registration card*. Until we receive your registration card, you have an unregistered system. Even if you have previously sent a card to us, please fill out and return the card enclosed in your Regression Models package. Registering your system entitles you to:

- Technical support services
- New product announcements and upgrade announcements

Customer Service

If you have any questions concerning your shipment or account, contact your local office, listed on page vi. Please have your serial number ready for identification when calling.

Training Seminars

SPSS Inc. provides both public and onsite training seminars for SPSS. All seminars feature hands-on workshops. SPSS seminars will be offered in major U.S. and European cities on a regular basis. For more information on these seminars, call your local office, listed on page vi.

Technical Support

The services of SPSS Technical Support are available to registered customers. Customers may call Technical Support for assistance in using SPSS products or for installation help for one of the supported hardware environments. To reach Technical Support, see the SPSS home page on the World Wide Web at *http://www.spss.com*, or call your local office, listed on page vi. Be prepared to identify yourself, your organization, and the serial number of your system.

Additional Publications

Additional copies of SPSS product manuals may be purchased from Prentice Hall, the exclusive distributor of SPSS publications. To order, fill out and mail the Publications order form included with your system or call toll-free. If you represent a bookstore or have an account with Prentice Hall, call 1-800-223-1360. If you are not an account customer, call 1-800-374-1200. In Canada, call 1-800-567-3800. Outside of North America, contact your local Prentice Hall office.

Except for academic course adoptions, manuals can also be purchased from SPSS Inc. Contact your local SPSS office, listed on page vi.

Tell Us Your Thoughts

Your comments are important. Please send us a letter and let us know about your experiences with SPSS products. We especially like to hear about new and interesting applications using the SPSS system. Write to SPSS Inc. Marketing Department, Attn: Director of Product Planning, 233 South Wacker Drive, 11th Floor, Chicago, IL 60606-6307.

About This Manual

This manual is divided into two sections. The first section documents the graphical user interface. Illustrations of dialog boxes are taken from SPSS for Windows. Dialog boxes in other operating systems are similar. In addition, this section provides examples of statistical procedures and advice on interpreting the output. The second part of the manual is a Syntax Reference section that provides complete command syntax for all of the commands included in the Regression Models option. The Regression Models command syntax is also available online with the CD-ROM version of SPSS.

This manual contains two indexes: a subject index and a syntax index. The subject index covers both sections of the manual. The syntax index applies only to the Syntax Reference section.

Contacting SPSS

If you would like to be on our mailing list, contact one of our offices, listed on page vi, or visit our WWW site at *http://www.spss.com*. We will send you a copy of our newsletter and let you know about SPSS Inc. activities in your area.

SPSS Inc.
Chicago, Illinois, U.S.A.
Tel: 1.312.651.3000
www.spss.com/corpinfo
Customer Service:
1.800.521.1337
Sales:
1.800.543.2185
sales@spss.com
Training:
1.800.543.6607
Technical Support:
1.312.651.3410
support@spss.com

SPSS Federal Systems
Tel: 1.703.527.6777
www.spss.com

SPSS Argentina srl
Tel: +541.814.5030
www.spss.com

SPSS Asia Pacific Pte. Ltd.
Tel: +65.245.9110
www.spss.com

SPSS Australasia Pty. Ltd.
Tel: +61.2.9954.5660
www.spss.com

SPSS Belgium
Tel: +32.162.389.82
www.spss.com

SPSS Benelux BV
Tel: +31.183.636711
www.spss.nl

**SPSS Central and
Eastern Europe**
Tel: +44.(0)1483.719200
www.spss.com

SPSS Czech Republic
Tel: +420.2.24813839
www.spss.cz

SPSS East Mediterranea and Africa
Tel: +972.9.8655747
www.spss.com

SPSS Finland Oy
Tel: +358.9.524.801
www.spss.com

SPSS France SARL
Tel: +33.1.5535.2700
www.spss.com

SPSS Germany
Tel: +49.89.4890740
www.spss.com

SPSS Hellas SA
Tel: +30.1.7251925/7251950
www.spss.com

SPSS Hispanoportuguesa S.L.
Tel: +34.91.447.37.00
www.spss.com

SPSS Ireland
Tel: +353.1.496.9007
www.spss.com

SPSS Israel Ltd.
Tel: +972.9.9526700
www.spss.com

SPSS Italia srl
Tel: +39.51.252573
www.spss.it

SPSS Japan Inc.
Tel: +81.3.5466.5511
www.spss.co.jp

SPSS Kenya Limited
Tel: +254.2.577.262
www.spss.com

SPSS Korea KIC Co., Ltd.
Tel: +82.2.3446.7651
www.spss.co.kr

SPSS Latin America
Tel: 1.312.494.3226
www.spss.com
SPSS Malaysia Sdn Bhd
Tel: +60.3.704.5877
www.spss.com

SPSS Mexico SA de CV
Tel: +52.5.682.87.68
www.spss.com

**SPSS Middle East and
South Asia**
Tel: +91.80.227.7436/221.8962
www.spss.com

SPSS Norway
Tel: +47.2254.0060
www.spss.com

SPSS Polska
Tel: +48.12.6369680
www.companion.krakow.pl

SPSS Russia
Tel: +7.095.125.0069
www.spss.com

SPSS Scandinavia AB
Tel: +46.8.506.105.50
www.spss.com

SPSS Schweiz AG
Tel: +41.1.266.90.30
www.spss.com

SPSS Singapore Pte. Ltd.
Tel: +65.533.3190
www.spss.com

SPSS South Africa
Tel: +27.11.807.3189
www.spss.com

SPSS Taiwan Corp.
Taipei, Republic of China
Tel: +886.2.25771100
www.spss.com

Contents

1 Choosing a Procedure for Binary Logistic Regression Models

Binary logistic regression models can be fitted using either the Logistic Regression procedure or the Multinomial Logistic Regression procedure. Each procedure has options not available in the other. An important theoretical distinction is that the Logistic Regression procedure produces all predictions, residuals, influence statistics, and goodness-of-fit tests using data at the individual case level, regardless of how the data are entered and whether or not the number of covariate patterns is smaller than the total number of cases, while the Multinomial Logistic Regression procedure internally aggregates cases to form subpopulations with identical covariate patterns for the predictors, producing predictions, residuals, and goodness-of-fit tests based on these subpopulations. If all predictors are categorical or any continuous predictors take on only a limited number of values—so that there are several cases at each distinct covariate pattern—the subpopulation approach can produce valid goodness of fit tests and informative residuals, while the individual case level approach cannot.

Logistic Regression provides the following unique features:

- Hosmer-Lemeshow test of goodness of fit for the model
- Stepwise analyses
- Contrasts to define model parameterization
- Alternative cut points for classification
- Classification plots
- Model fitted on one set of cases to a held-out set of cases
- Saves predictions, residuals, and influence statistics

Multinomial Logistic Regression provides the following unique features:

- Pearson and deviance chi-square tests for goodness of fit of the model
- Specification of subpopulations for grouping of data for goodness-of-fit tests
- Listing of counts, predicted counts, and residuals by subpopulations
- Correction of variance estimates for over-dispersion
- Covariance matrix of the parameter estimates

- Tests of linear combinations of parameters
- Explicit specification of nested models
- Fit 1-1 matched conditional logistic regression models using differenced variables

2

Logistic Regression

Logistic regression is useful for situations in which you want to be able to predict the presence or absence of a characteristic or outcome based on values of a set of predictor variables. It is similar to a linear regression model but is suited to models where the dependent variable is dichotomous. Logistic regression coefficients can be used to estimate odds ratios for each of the independent variables in the model. Logistic regression is applicable to a broader range of research situations than discriminant analysis.

Example. What lifestyle characteristics are risk factors for coronary heart disease (CHD)? Given a sample of patients measured on smoking status, diet, exercise, alcohol use, and CHD status, you could build a model using the four lifestyle variables to predict the presence or absence of CHD in a sample of patients. The model can then be used to derive estimates of the odds ratios for each factor to tell you, for example, how much more likely smokers are to develop CHD than nonsmokers.

Statistics. For each analysis: total cases, selected cases, valid cases. For each categorical variable: parameter coding. For each step: variable(s) entered or removed, iteration history, -2 log-likelihood, goodness of fit, Hosmer-Lemeshow goodness-of-fit statistic, model chi-square, improvement chi-square, classification table, correlations between variables, observed groups and predicted probabilities chart, residual chi-square. For each variable in the equation: coefficient (B), standard error of B, Wald statistic, R, estimated odds ratio ($\exp(B)$), confidence interval for $\exp(B)$, log-likelihood if term removed from model. For each variable not in the equation: score statistic, R. For each case: observed group, predicted probability, predicted group, residual, standardized residual.

Methods. You can estimate models using block entry of variables or any of the following stepwise methods: forward conditional, forward LR, forward Wald, backward conditional, backward LR, or backward Wald.

Data. The dependent variable should be dichotomous. Independent variables can be interval level or categorical; if categorical, they should be dummy or indicator coded (there is an option in the procedure to recode categorical variables automatically).

Assumptions. Logistic regression does not rely on distributional assumptions in the same sense that discriminant analysis does. However, your solution may be more stable if your predictors have a multivariate normal distribution. Additionally, as with other forms of regression, multicollinearity among the predictors can lead to biased estimates and inflated standard errors. The procedure is most effective when group membership is a truly categorical variable; if group membership is based on values of a continuous variable (for example, "high IQ" versus "low IQ"), you should consider using linear regression to take advantage of the richer information offered by the continuous variable itself.

Related procedures. Use the Scatterplot procedure to screen your data for multicollinearity. If assumptions of multivariate normality and equal variance-covariance matrices are met, you may be able to get a quicker solution using the Discriminant Analysis procedure. If all of your predictor variables are categorical, you can also use the Loglinear procedure. If your dependent variable is continuous, use the Linear Regression procedure.

To Obtain a Logistic Regression Analysis

▶ From the menus choose:

Analyze
 Regression
  Binary Logistic...

Figure 2.1   Expanded Logistic Regression dialog box

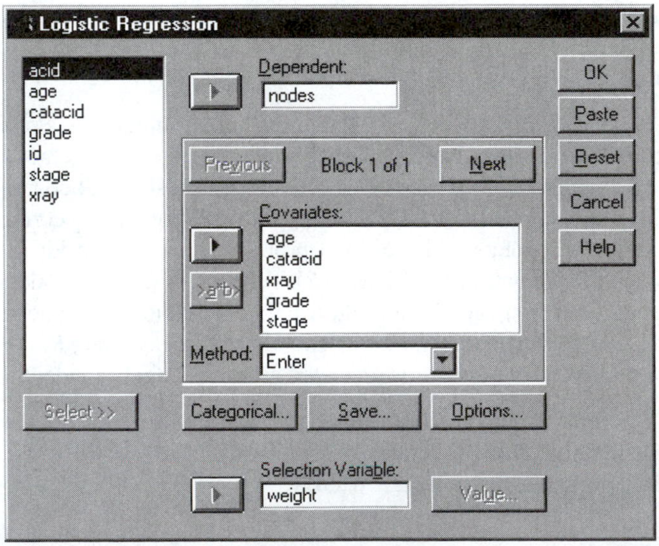

▶ Select one dichotomous dependent variable. This variable may be numeric or short string.

▶ Select one or more covariates. To include interaction terms, select all of the variables involved in the interaction and then select >*a*b*>.

▶ To enter variables in groups (blocks), select the covariates for a block, and click *Next* to specify a new block. Repeat until all blocks have been specified.

Optionally, you can select cases for analysis. Click *Select*, choose a selection variable, and click *Rule*.

Logistic Regression Set Rule

Figure 2.2   Logistic Regression Set Rule dialog box

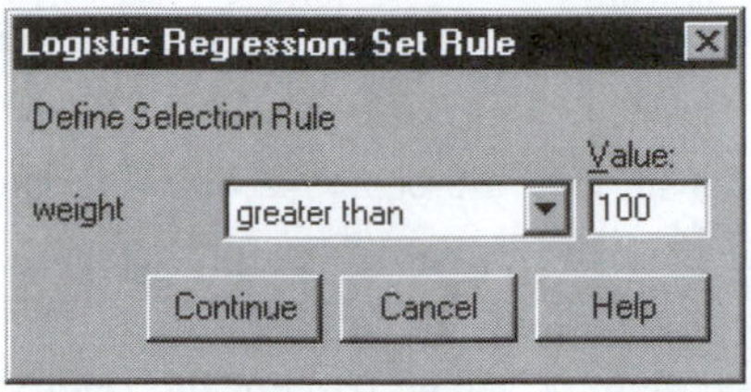

Cases defined by the selection rule are included in the model estimation. For example, if you selected a variable and *equals* and specified a value of 5, then only the cases for which the selected variable has a value equal to 5 are included in the model estimation.

Statistics and classification results are generated for both selected and unselected cases. This provides a mechanism for classifying new cases based on previously existing data, or for partitioning your data into training and testing subsets, to perform validation on the model generated.

Logistic Regression Define Categorical Variables

Figure 2.3   Logistic Regression Define Categorical Variables dialog box

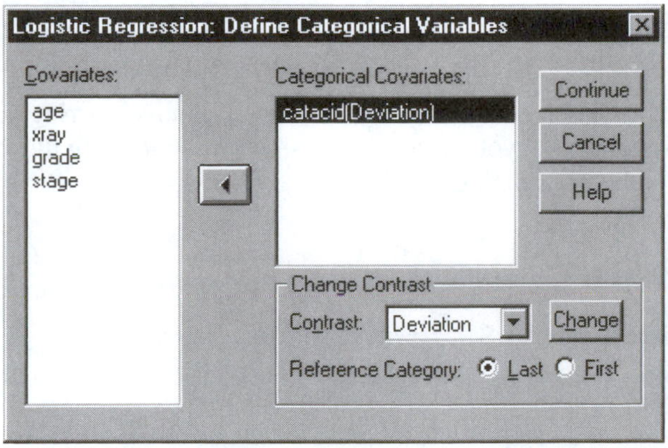

You can specify details of how the Logistic Regression procedure will handle categorical variables:

Covariates. Contains a list of all of the covariates specified in the main dialog box, either by themselves or as part of an interaction, in any layer. If some of these are string variables or are categorical, you can use them only as categorical covariates.

Categorical Covariates. Lists variables identified as categorical. Each variable includes a notation in parentheses indicating the contrast coding to be used. String variables (denoted by the symbol < following their names) are already present in the Categorical Covariates list. Select any other categorical covariates from the Covariates list and move them into the Categorical Covariates list.

Change Contrast. Allows you to change the contrast method. Available contrast methods are:

- **Deviation.** Each category of the predictor variable except the reference category is compared to the overall effect.

- **Simple.** Each category of the predictor variable (except the reference category) is compared to the reference category.

- **Difference.** Each category of the predictor variable except the first category is compared to the average effect of previous categories. Also known as reverse Helmert contrasts.

- **Helmert.** Each category of the predictor variable except the last category is compared to the average effect of subsequent categories.

- **Repeated.** Each category of the predictor variable except the first category is compared to the category that precedes it.

- **Polynomial.** Orthogonal polynomial contrasts. Categories are assumed to be equally spaced. Polynomial contrasts are available for numeric variables only.

- **Indicator.** Contrasts indicate the presence or absence of category membership. The reference category is represented in the contrast matrix as a row of zeros.

If you select *Deviation*, *Simple*, or *Indicator*, select either *First* or *Last* as the reference category. Note that the method is not actually changed until you click *Change*.

String covariates *must* be categorical covariates. To remove a string variable from the Categorical Covariates list, you must remove all terms containing the variable from the Covariates list in the main dialog box.

Logistic Regression Save New Variables

Figure 2.4   Logistic Regression Save New Variables dialog box

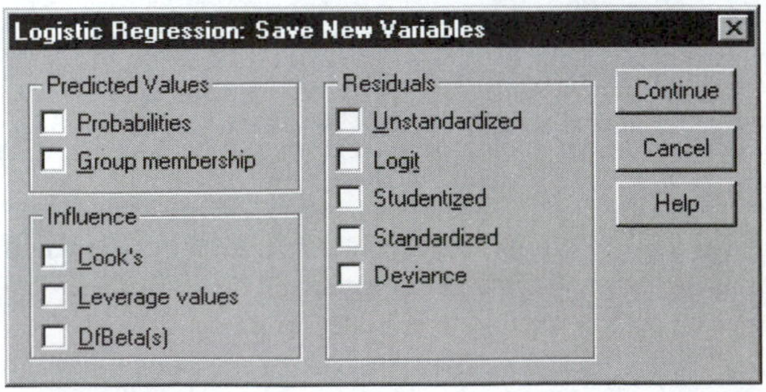

You can save results of the logistic regression as new variables in the working data file:

Predicted Values. Saves values predicted by the model. Available options are Probabilities and Group membership.

Influence. Saves values from statistics that measure the influence of cases on predicted values. Available options are Cook's, Leverage values, and DfBeta(s).

Residuals. Saves residuals. Available options are Unstandardized, Logit, Studentized, Standardized, and Deviance.

Logistic Regression Options

Figure 2.5   Logistic Regression Options dialog box

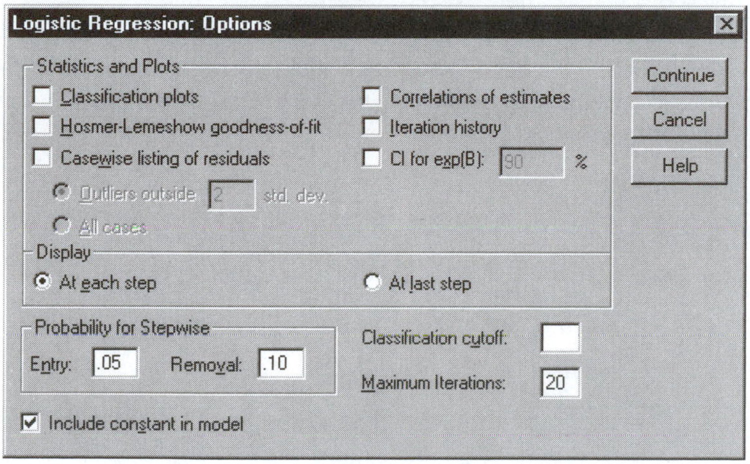

You can specify options for your logistic regression analysis:

Statistics and Plots. Allows you to request statistics and plots. Available options are Classification plots, Hosmer-Lemeshow goodness-of-fit, Casewise listing of residuals, Correlations of estimates, Iteration history, and CI for exp(B). Select one of the alternatives in the Display group to display statistics and plots either At each step or, only for the final model, At last step.

Probability for Stepwise. Allows you to control the criteria by which variables are entered into and removed from the equation. You can specify criteria for entry or removal of variables.

Classification cutoff. Allows you to determine the cut point for classifying cases. Cases with predicted values that exceed the classification cutoff are classified as positive, while those with predicted values smaller than the cutoff are classified as negative. To change the default, enter a value between 0.01 and 0.99.

Maximum Iterations. Allows you to change the maximum number of times that the model iterates before terminating.

Include constant in model. Allows you to indicate whether the model should include a constant term. If disabled, the constant term will equal 0.

LOGISTIC REGRESSION Command Additional Features

The SPSS command language also allows you to:

- Identify casewise output by the values or variable labels of a variable.
- Control the spacing of iteration reports. Rather than printing parameter estimates after every iteration, you can request parameter estimates after every nth iteration.
- Change the criteria for terminating iteration and checking for redundancy.
- Specify a variable list for casewise listings.
- Conserve memory by holding the data for each split-file group in an external scratch file during processing.

3 Multinomial Logistic Regression

Multinomial Logistic Regression is useful for situations in which you want to be able to classify subjects based on values of a set of predictor variables. This type of regression is similar to logistic regression, but it is more general because the dependent variable is not restricted to two categories.

Example. In order to market films more effectively, movie studios want to predict what type of film a moviegoer is likely to see. By performing a Multinomial Logistic Regression, the studio can determine the strength of influence a person's age, gender, and dating status has upon the type of film they prefer. The studio can then slant the advertising campaign of a particular movie towards a group of people likely to go see it.

Statistics. Iteration history, parameter coefficients, asymptotic covariance and correlation matrices, likelihood-ratio tests for model and partial effects, -2 log-likelihood. Pearson and deviance chi-square goodness of fit. Cox and Snell, Nagelkerke, and McFadden R^2. Classification: observed versus predicted frequencies by response category. Crosstabulation: observed and predicted frequencies (with residuals) and proportions by covariate pattern and response category.

Methods. A multinomial logit model is fit for the full factorial model, or a user-specified model. Parameter estimation is performed through an iterative maximum-likelihood algorithm.

Data. The dependent variable should be categorical. Independent variables can be factors or covariates. In general, factors should be categorical variables and covariates should be continuous variables.

Assumptions. It is assumed that the odds ratio of any two categories are independent of all other response categories. For example, if a new product is introduced to a market, this assumption states that the market shares of all other products are affected proportionally equally. Also, given a covariate pattern, the responses are assumed to be independent multinomial variables.

To Obtain a Multinomial Logistic Regression

▶ From the menus choose:

Analyze
 Regression
  Multinomial Logistic...

Figure 3.1   Multinomial Logistic Regression dialog box

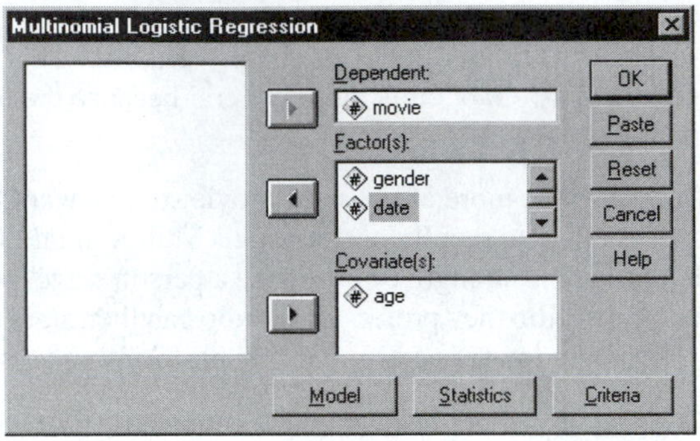

▶ Select one dependent variable.

▶ Factors are optional and can be either numeric or categorical.

▶ Covariates are optional but must be numeric if specified.

Multinomial Logistic Regression Models

Figure 3.2   Multinomial Logistic Regression Model dialog box

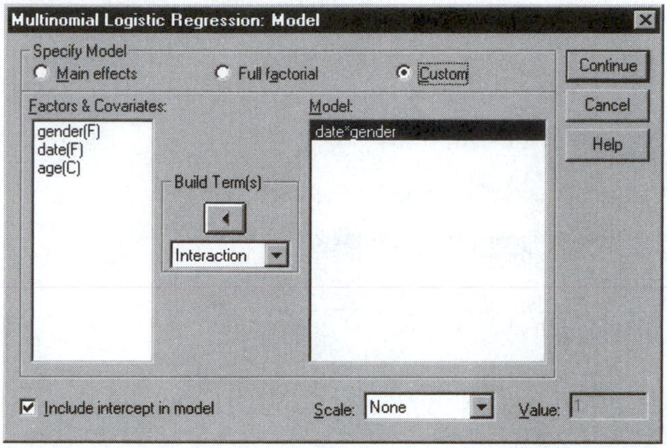

You can specify the following models for your Multinomial Logistic Regression:

Specify Model. A main-effects model contains the covariate and factor main effects but no interaction effects. A full factorial model contains all main effects and all factor-by-factor interactions. It does not contain covariate interactions. You can create a custom model to specify subsets of factor interactions or covariate interactions.

Factors and Covariates. The factors and covariates are listed with (F) for factor and (C) for covariate.

Model. The model depends on the main and interaction effects you select.

Include intercept in model. Allows you to include or exclude an intercept term for the model.

Scale. Allows you to specify the dispersion scaling value that will be used to correct the estimate of the parameter covariance matrix. **Deviance** estimates the scaling value using the deviance function (likelihood-ratio chi-square) statistic. **Pearson** estimates the scaling value using the Pearson chi-square statistic. You can also specify your own scaling value. It must be a positive numeric value.

Build Terms

For the selected factors and covariates:

Main effects. Creates a main-effects term for each variable selected.

Interaction. Creates the highest-level interaction term of all selected variables.

All 2-way. Creates all possible two-way interactions of the selected variables.

All 3-way. Creates all possible three-way interactions of the selected variables.

All 4-way. Creates all possible four-way interactions of the selected variables.

All 5-way. Creates all possible five-way interactions of the selected variables.

Multinomial Logistic Regression Statistics

Figure 3.3   Multinomial Logistic Regression Statistics dialog box

You can specify the following statistics for your Multinomial Logistic Regression:

Summary statistics. Prints the Cox and Snell, Nagelkerke, and McFadden R^2 statistics.

Likelihood ratio test. Prints likelihood-ratio tests for the model partial effects. The test for the overall model is printed automatically.

Parameter estimates. Prints estimates of the model effects, with a user-specified level of confidence.

Asymptotic correlation of parameter estimates. Prints matrix of parameter estimate correlations.

Asymptotic covariance of parameter estimates. Prints matrix of parameter estimate covariances.

Cell probabilities. Prints a table of the observed and expected frequencies (with residual) and proportions by covariate pattern and response category.

Classification table. Prints a table of the observed versus predicted responses.

Goodness of fit chi-square statistics. Prints Pearson and likelihood-ratio chi-square statistics. Statistics are computed for the covariate patterns determined by all factors and covariates or by a user-defined subset of the factors and covariates.

Define Subpopulations. Allows you to select a subset of the factors and covariates in order to define the covariate patterns used by cell probabilities and the goodness-of-fit tests.

Multinomial Logistic Regression Convergence Criteria

Figure 3.4   Multinomial Logistic Regression Convergence Criteria dialog box

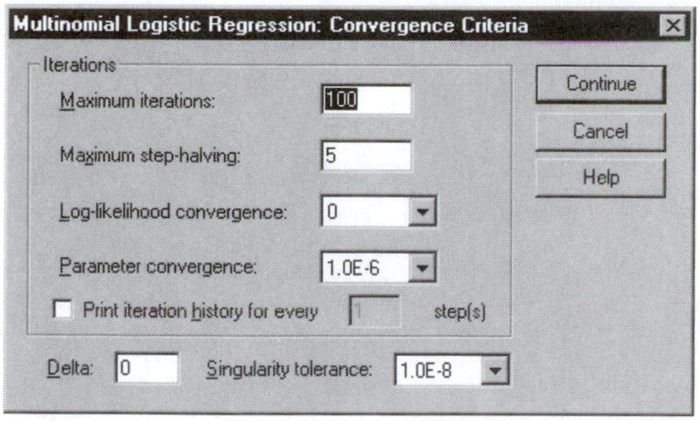

You can specify the following criteria for your Multinomial Logistic Regression:

Iterations. Allows you to specify the maximum number of times you want to cycle through the algorithm, the maximum number of steps in the step-halving, the convergence tolerances for changes in the log-likelihood and parameters, and how often the progress of the iterative algorithm is printed.

Delta. Allows you to specify a non-negative value less than 1. This value is added to each cell in the crosstabulation of response category by covariate pattern. This is useful when some cells have zero observations.

Singularity tolerance. Allows you to specify the tolerance used in checking for singularities.

NOMREG Command Additional Features

The SPSS command language also allows you to:

- Include cases with user-missing values.
- Customize hypothesis tests by specifying null hypotheses as linear combinations of parameters.

4 Probit Analysis

This procedure measures the relationship between the strength of a stimulus and the proportion of cases exhibiting a certain response to the stimulus. It is useful for situations where you have a dichotomous output that is thought to be influenced or caused by levels of some independent variable(s) and is particularly well suited to experimental data. This procedure will allow you to estimate the strength of a stimulus required to induce a certain proportion of responses, such as the median effective dose.

This procedure uses the algorithms proposed and implemented in NPSOL ® by Gill, Murray, Saunders & Wright to estimate the model parameters.

Example. How effective is a new pesticide at killing ants, and what is an appropriate concentration to use? You might perform an experiment in which you expose samples of ants to different concentrations of the pesticide and then record the number of ants killed and the number of ants exposed. Applying probit analysis to these data, you can determine the strength of the relationship between concentration and killing, and you can determine what the appropriate concentration of pesticide would be if you wanted to be sure to kill, say, 95% of exposed ants.

Statistics. Regression coefficients and standard errors, intercept and standard error, Pearson goodness-of-fit chi-square, observed and expected frequencies, and confidence intervals for effective levels of independent variable(s). Plots: transformed response plots.

Data. For each value of the independent variable (or each combination of values for multiple independent variables), your response variable should be a count of the number of cases with those values that show the response of interest, and the total observed variable should be a count of the total number of cases with those values for the independent variable. The factor variable should be categorical, coded as integers.

Assumptions. Observations should be independent. If you have a large number of values for the independent variables relative to the number of observations, as you might in an observational study, the chi-square and goodness-of-fit statistics may not be valid.

Related procedures. Probit analysis is closely related to logistic regression; in fact, if you choose the logit transformation, this procedure will essentially compute a logistic regression. In general, probit analysis is appropriate for designed experiments, whereas logistic regression is more appropriate for observational studies. The differences in output reflect these different emphases. The probit analysis procedure reports estimates of effective values for various rates of response (including median effective dose), while the logistic regression procedure reports estimates of odds ratios for independent variables.

To Obtain a Probit Analysis

▶ From the menus choose:

Analyze
  Regression
    Probit...

Figure 4.1   Probit Analysis dialog box

▶ Select a response frequency variable. This variable indicates the number of cases exhibiting a response to the test stimulus. The values of this variable cannot be negative.

▶ Select a total observed variable. This variable indicates the number of cases to which the stimulus was applied. The values of this variable cannot be negative and cannot be less than the values of the response frequency variable for each case.

  Optionally, you can select a factor variable. If you do, click *Define Range* to define the groups.

▶ Select one or more covariate(s). This variable contains the level of the stimulus applied to each observation. If you want to transform the covariate, select a transformation from the Transform drop-down list. If no transformation is applied, and there is a control group, then the control group is included in the analysis.

▶ Select either *Probit* or *Logit* model.

Probit Analysis Define Range

Figure 4.2   Probit Analysis Define Range dialog box

This allows you to specify the levels of the factor variable that will be analyzed. The factor levels must be coded as consecutive integers, and all levels in the range you specify will be analyzed.

Probit Analysis Options

Figure 4.3   Probit Analysis Options dialog box

You can specify options for your probit analysis:

Statistics. Allows you to request the following optional statistics: Frequencies, Relative median potency, Parallelism test, and Fiducial confidence intervals.

Fiducial confidence intervals and Relative median potency are unavailable if you have selected more than one covariate. Relative median potency and Parallelism test are available only if you have selected a factor variable.

Natural Response Rate. Allows you to indicate a natural response rate even in the absence of the stimulus. Available alternatives are None, Calculate from data, or Value.

Criteria. Allows you to control parameters of the iterative parameter-estimation algorithm. You can override the defaults for maximum iterations, step limit, and optimality tolerance.

PROBIT Command Additional Features

The SPSS command language also allows you to:
- Request an analysis on both the probit and logit models.
- Control the treatment of missing values.
- Transform the covariates by bases other than base 10 or natural log.

5 Nonlinear Regression

Nonlinear regression is a method of finding a nonlinear model of the relationship between the dependent variable and a set of independent variables. Unlike traditional linear regression, which is restricted to estimating linear models, nonlinear regression can estimate models with arbitrary relationships between independent and dependent variables. This is accomplished using iterative estimation algorithms. Note that this procedure is not necessary for simple polynomial models of the form $Y = A + BX**2$. By defining $W = X**2$, we get a simple linear model, $Y = A + BW$, which can be estimated using traditional methods such as the Linear Regression procedure.

Constrained nonlinear regression uses the algorithms proposed and implemented in NPSOL® by Gill, Murray, Saunders, and Wright to estimate the model parameters.

Example. Can population be predicted based on time? A scatterplot shows that there seems to be a strong relationship between population and time, but the relationship is nonlinear, so it requires the special estimation methods of the Nonlinear Regression procedure. By setting up an appropriate equation, such as a logistic population growth model, we can get a good estimate of the model, allowing us to make predictions about population for times that were not actually measured.

Statistics. For each iteration: parameter estimates and residual sum of squares. For each model: sum of squares for regression, residual, uncorrected total and corrected total, parameter estimates, asymptotic standard errors, and asymptotic correlation matrix of parameter estimates.

Data. The dependent and independent variables should be quantitative. Categorical variables such as religion, major, or region of residence need to be recoded to binary (dummy) variables or other types of contrast variables.

Assumptions. Results are valid only if you have specified a function that accurately describes the relationship between dependent and independent variables. Additionally, the choice of good starting values is very important. Even if you've specified the correct functional form of the model, if you use poor starting values, your model may fail to converge or you may get a locally optimal solution rather than one that is globally optimal.

Related procedures. Many models that appear nonlinear at first can be transformed to a linear model, which can be analyzed using the Linear Regression procedure. If you are uncertain what the proper model should be, the Curve Estimation procedure can help to identify useful functional relations in your data.

To Obtain a Nonlinear Regression Analysis

▶ From the menus choose:

Analyze
  Regression
    Nonlinear…

Figure 5.1   Nonlinear Regression dialog box

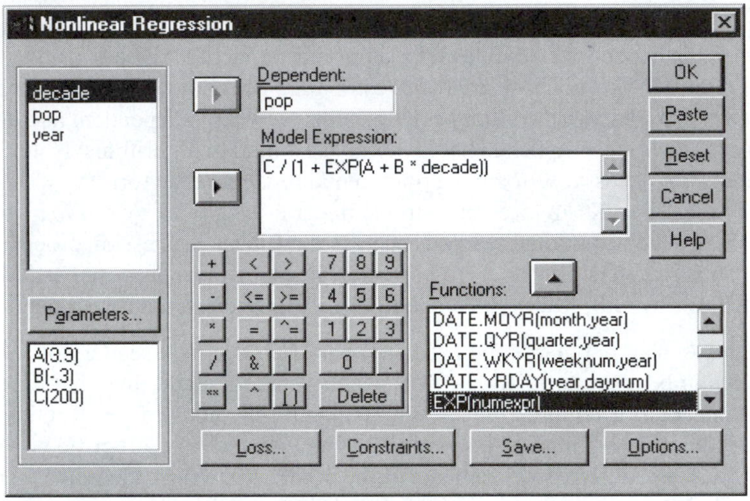

▶ Select one numeric dependent variable from the list of variables in your working data file.

▶ To build a model expression, enter the expression in the Model field or paste components (variables, parameters, functions) into the field.

▶ Identify parameters in your model by clicking *Parameters*.

A segmented model (one that takes different forms in different parts of its domain) must be specified by using *conditional logic* within the single model statement.

Conditional Logic (Nonlinear Regression)

You can specify a segmented model using conditional logic. To use conditional logic within a model expression or a loss function, you form the sum of a series of terms, one for each condition. Each term consists of a logical expression (in parentheses) multiplied by the expression that should result when that logical expression is true.

For example, consider a segmented model that equals 0 for $X <= 0$, X for $0 < X < 1$, and 1 for $X >= 1$. The expression for this is:

$(X <= 0)*0 + (X > 0 \ \& \ X < 1)*X + (X >= 1)*1.$

The logical expressions in parentheses all evaluate to 1 (true) or 0 (false). Therefore:

If $X <= 0$, the above reduces to $1*0 + 0*X + 0*1 = 0$.

If $0 < X < 1$, it reduces to $0*0 + 1*X + 0*1 = X$.

If $X >= 1$, it reduces to $0*0 + 0*X + 1*1 = 1$.

More complicated examples can be easily built by substituting different logical expressions and outcome expressions. Remember that double inequalities, such as $0 < X < 1$, must be written as compound expressions, such as $(X > 0 \ \& \ X < 1)$.

String variables can be used within logical expressions:

(city = 'New York')*costliv + (city = 'Des Moines')*0.59*costliv

This yields one expression (the value of the variable *costliv*) for New Yorkers and another (59% of that value) for Des Moines residents. String constants must be enclosed in quotation marks or apostrophes, as shown here.

Nonlinear Regression Parameters

Figure 5.2   Nonlinear Regression Parameters dialog box

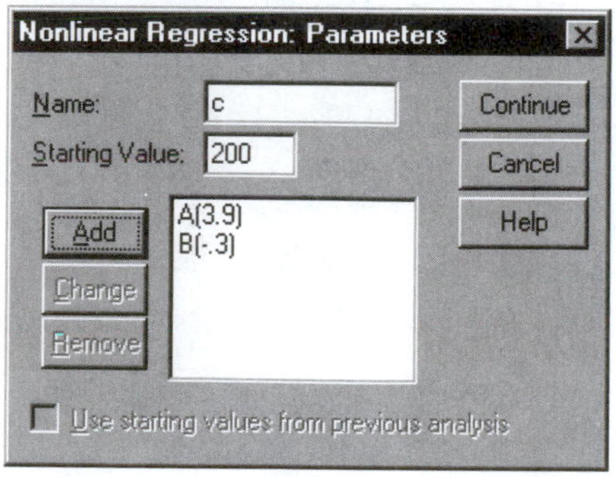

Parameters are the parts of your model that the Nonlinear Regression procedure estimates. Parameters can be additive constants, multiplicative coefficients, exponents, or values used in evaluating functions. All parameters that you have defined will appear (with their initial values) on the Parameters list in the main dialog box.

Name. You must specify a name for each parameter. This name must be a valid SPSS variable name and must be the name used in the model expression in the main dialog box.

Starting Value. Allows you to specify a starting value for the parameter, preferably as close as possible to the expected final solution. Poor starting values can result in failure to converge or in convergence on a solution that is local (rather than global) or is physically impossible.

Use starting values from previous analysis. If you have already run a nonlinear regression from this dialog box, you can select this option to obtain the initial values of parameters from their values in the previous run. This permits you to continue searching when the algorithm is converging slowly. (The initial starting values will still appear on the Parameters list in the main dialog box.) *Note:* This selection persists in this dialog box for the rest of your session. *If you change the model, be sure to deselect it.*

Nonlinear Regression Common Models

The table below provides example model syntax for many published nonlinear regression models. *A model selected at random is not likely to fit your data well.* Appropriate starting values for the parameters are necessary, and some models require constraints in order to converge.

Table 5.1   Example model syntax

Name	Model expression
Asymptotic Regression	b1 + b2 *exp(b3 * x)
Asymptotic Regression	b1 −(b2 *(b3 ** x))
Density	(b1 + b2 * x)**(−1/ b3)
Gauss	b1 *(1− b3 *exp(−b2 * x **2))
Gompertz	b1 *exp(−b2 * exp(−b3 * x))
Johnson-Schumacher	b1 *exp(−b2 / (x + b3))
Log-Modified	(b1 + b3 * x) ** b2
Log-Logistic	b1 −ln(1+ b2 *exp(−b3 * x))
Metcherlich Law of Diminishing Returns	b1 + b2 *exp(−b3 * x)
Michaelis Menten	b1* x /(x + b2)
Morgan-Mercer-Florin	(b1 * b2 + b3 * x ** b4)/(b2 + x ** b4)
Peal-Reed	b1 /(1+ b2 *exp(−(b3 * x + b4 * x **2+ b5 * x **3)))
Ratio of Cubics	(b1 + b2 * x + b3 * x **2+ b4 * x **3)/(b5 * x **3)
Ratio of Quadratics	(b1 + b2 * x + b3 * x **2)/(b4 * x **2)
Richards	b1 /((1+ b3 *exp(− b2 * x))**(1/ b4))
Verhulst	b1 /(1 + b3 * exp(− b2 * x))
Von Bertalanffy	(b1 ** (1 − b4) − b2 * exp(−b3 * x)) ** (1/(1 − b4))
Weibull	b1 − b2 *exp(− b3 * x ** b4)
Yield Density	(b1 + b2 * x + b3 * x **2)**(−1)

Nonlinear Regression Loss Function

Figure 5.3   Nonlinear Regression Loss Function dialog box

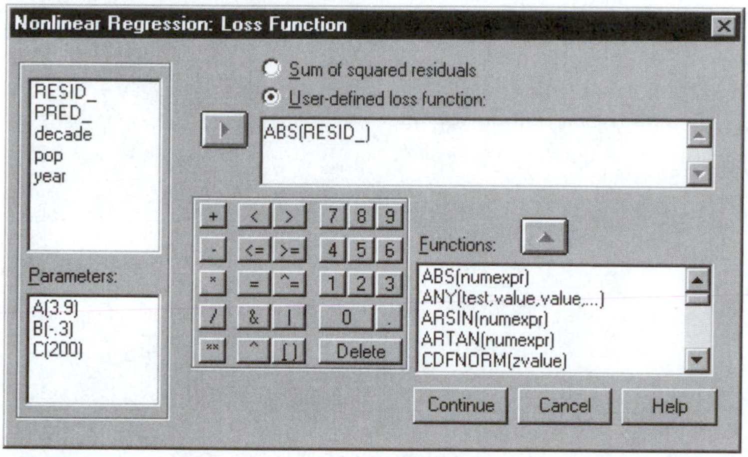

The **loss function** in nonlinear regression is the function that is minimized by the algorithm. Select either *Sum of squared residuals* to minimize the sum of the squared residuals or *User-defined loss function* to minimize a different function.

If you select *User-defined loss function*, you must define the loss function whose sum (across all cases) should be minimized by the choice of parameter values.

- Most loss functions involve the special variable *RESID_*, which represents the residual. (The default *Sum of squared residuals* loss function could be entered explicitly as RESID_**2.) If you need to use the predicted value in your loss function, it is equal to the dependent variable minus the residual.

- It is possible to specify a *conditional loss function* using conditional logic.

You can either type an expression in the User-defined loss function field or paste components of the expression into the field. String constants must be enclosed in quotation marks or apostrophes, and numeric constants must be typed in American format, with the dot as a decimal delimiter.

Nonlinear Regression Parameter Constraints

Figure 5.4   Nonlinear Regression Parameter Constraints dialog box

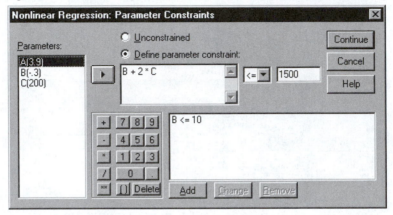

A **constraint** is a restriction on the allowable values for a parameter during the iterative search for a solution. Linear expressions are evaluated before a step is taken, so you can use linear constraints to prevent steps that might result in overflows. Nonlinear expressions are evaluated after a step is taken.

Each equation or inequality requires the following elements:

- An expression *involving at least one parameter* in the model. Type the expression or use the keypad, which allows you to paste numbers, operators, or parentheses into the expression. You can either type in the required parameter(s) along with the rest of the expression or paste from the Parameters list at the left. You cannot use ordinary variables in a constraint.
- One of the three logical operators <=, =, or >=.
- A numeric constant, to which the expression is compared using the logical operator. Type the constant. Numeric constants must be typed in American format, with the dot as a decimal delimiter.

Nonlinear Regression Save New Variables

Figure 5.5   Nonlinear Regression Save New Variables dialog box

Nonlinear Regression: Save New

☐ Predicted values
☐ Residuals
☐ Derivatives
☐ Loss function values

Continue
Cancel
Help

You can save a number of new variables to your active data file. Available options are Predicted values, Residuals, Derivatives, and Loss function values. These variables can be used in subsequent analyses to test the fit of the model or to identify problem cases.

Nonlinear Regression Options

Figure 5.6   Nonlinear Regression Options dialog box

Options allow you to control various aspects of your nonlinear regression analysis:

Bootstrap estimates of standard error. Requests bootstrap estimates of the standard errors for parameters. This requires the sequential quadratic programming algorithm.

Estimation Method. Allows you to select an estimation method, if possible. (Certain choices in this or other dialog boxes require the sequential quadratic programming algorithm.) Available alternatives include Sequential quadratic programming and Levenberg-Marquardt.

Sequential Quadratic Programming. Allows you to specify options for this estimation method. You can enter new values for Maximum iterations and Step limit, and you can change the selection in the drop-down lists for Optimality tolerance, Function precision, and Infinite step size.

Levenberg-Marquardt. Allows you to specify options for this estimation process. You can enter new values for Maximum iterations, and you can change the selection in the drop-down lists for Sum-of-squares convergence and Parameter convergence.

Interpreting Nonlinear Regression Results

Nonlinear regression problems often present computational difficulties:

- The choice of initial values for the parameters influences convergence. Try to choose initial values that are reasonable and, if possible, close to the expected final solution.

- Sometimes one algorithm performs better than the other on a particular problem. In the Options dialog box, select the other algorithm if it is available. (If you specify a loss function or certain types of constraints, you cannot use the Levenberg-Marquardt algorithm.)

- When iteration stops only because the maximum number of iterations has occurred, the "final" model is probably not a good solution. Select *Use starting values from previous analysis* in the Parameters dialog box to continue the iteration or, better yet, choose different initial values.

- Models that require exponentiation of or by large data values can cause overflows or underflows (numbers too large or too small for the computer to represent). Sometimes you can avoid these by suitable choice of initial values or by imposing constraints on the parameters.

NLR Command Additional Features

The SPSS command language also allows you to:

- Name a file from which to read initial values for parameter estimates.
- Specify more than one model statement and loss function. This makes it easier to specify a segmented model.
- Supply your own derivatives rather than use those calculated by the program.
- Specify the number of bootstrap samples to generate.
- Specify additional iteration criteria, including setting a critical value for derivative checking and defining a convergence criterion for the correlation between the residuals and the derivatives.

Additional criteria for the CNLR (constrained nonlinear regression) command allow you to:

- Specify the maximum number of minor iterations allowed within each major iteration.
- Set a critical value for derivative checking.
- Set a step limit.
- Specify a crash tolerance to determine if initial values are within their specified bounds.

6 Weight Estimation

Standard linear regression models assume that variance is constant within the population under study. When this is not the case—for example, when cases that are high on some attribute show more variability than cases that are low on that attribute—linear regression using ordinary least squares (OLS) no longer provides optimal model estimates. If the differences in variability can be predicted from another variable, the Weight Estimation procedure can compute the coefficients of a linear regression model using weighted least squares (WLS), such that the more precise observations (that is, those with less variability) are given greater weight in determining the regression coefficients. The Weight Estimation procedure tests a range of weight transformations and indicates which will give the best fit to the data.

Example. What are the effects of inflation and unemployment on changes in stock prices? Because stocks with higher share values often show more variability than those with low share values, ordinary least squares will not produce optimal estimates. Weight estimation allows you to account for the effect of share price on the variability of price changes in calculating the linear model.

Statistics. Log-likelihood values for each power of the weight source variable tested, multiple R, R-squared, adjusted R-squared, ANOVA table for WLS model, unstandardized and standardized parameter estimates, and log-likelihood for the WLS model.

Data. The dependent and independent variables should be quantitative. Categorical variables such as religion, major, or region of residence need to be recoded to binary (dummy) variables or other types of contrast variables. The weight variable should be quantitative and should be related to the variability in the dependent variable.

Assumptions. For each value of the independent variable, the distribution of the dependent variable must be normal. The relationship between the dependent variable and each independent variable should be linear, and all observations should be independent. The variance of the dependent variable can vary across levels of the independent variable(s), but the differences must be predictable based on the weight variable.

Related procedures. The Explore procedure can be used to screen your data. Explore provides tests for normality and homogeneity of variance, as well as graphical displays. If your dependent variable seems to have equal variance across levels of independent variables, you can use the Linear Regression procedure. If your data appear to violate an assumption (such as normality), try transforming them. If your data are not related linearly and a transformation does not help, use an alternate model in the Curve Estimation procedure. If your dependent variable is dichotomous—for example, whether a particular sale is completed or whether an item is defective—use the Logistic Regression procedure. If your dependent variable is censored—for example, survival time after surgery—use Life Tables, Kaplan-Meier, or Cox Regression, available in the SPSS Advanced Models option. If your data are not independent—for example, if you observe the same person under several conditions—use the Repeated Measures procedure, available in the SPSS Advanced Models option.

To Obtain a Weight Estimation Analysis

▶   From the menus choose:

Analyze
  Regression
    Weight Estimation...

Figure 6.1   Weight Estimation dialog box

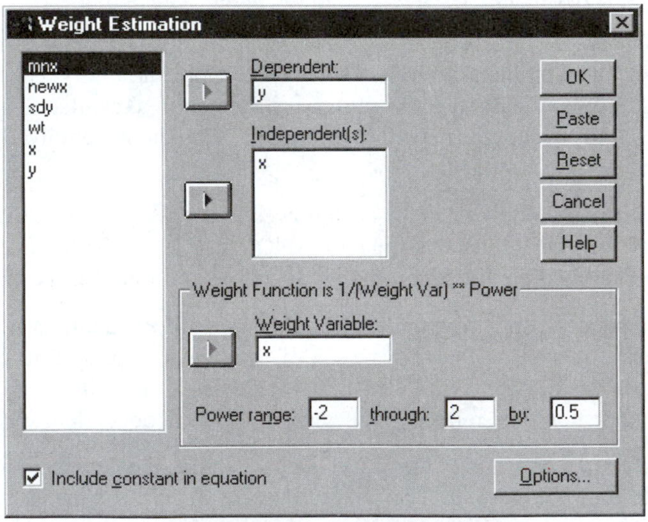

▶   Select one dependent variable.

▶   Select one or more independent variables.

▶   Select the variable that is the source of heteroscedasticity as the weight variable.

Weight Estimation Options

Figure 6.2   Weight Estimation Options dialog box

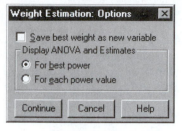

You can specify options for your weight estimation analysis:

Save best weight as new variable. Adds the weight variable to the active file. This variable is called *WGT_n*, where *n* is a number chosen to give the variable a unique name.

Display ANOVA and Estimates. Allows you to control how statistics are displayed in the output. Available alternatives are For best power and For each power value.

WLS Command Additional Features

The SPSS command language also allows you to:

• Provide a single value for the power.

• Specify a list of power values, or mix a range of values with a list of values for the power.

7 Two-Stage Least-Squares Regression

Standard linear regression models assume that errors in the dependent variable are uncorrelated with the independent variable(s). When this is not the case (for example, when relationships between variables are bidirectional), linear regression using ordinary least squares (OLS) no longer provides optimal model estimates. Two-stage least-squares regression uses instrumental variables that are uncorrelated with the error terms to compute estimated values of the problematic predictor(s) (the first stage), and then uses those computed values to estimate a linear regression model of the dependent variable (the second stage). Since the computed values are based on variables that are uncorrelated with the errors, the results of the two-stage model are optimal.

Example. Is the demand for a commodity related to its price and consumers' incomes? The difficulty in this model is that price and demand have a reciprocal effect on each other. That is, price can influence demand and demand can also influence price. A two-stage least-squares regression model might use consumers' incomes and lagged price to calculate a proxy for price that is uncorrelated with the measurement errors in demand. This proxy is substituted for price itself in the originally specified model, which is then estimated.

Statistics. For each model: standardized and unstandardized regression coefficients, multiple R, R-squared, adjusted R-squared, standard error of the estimate, analysis-of-variance table, predicted values, and residuals. Also, 95% confidence intervals for each regression coefficient, and correlation and covariance matrices of parameter estimates.

Data. The dependent and independent variables should be quantitative. Categorical variables, such as religion, major, or region of residence, need to be recoded to binary (dummy) variables or other types of contrast variables. Endogenous explanatory variables should be quantitative (not categorical).

Assumptions. For each value of the independent variable, the distribution of the dependent variable must be normal. The variance of the distribution of the dependent variable should be constant for all values of the independent variable. The relationship between the dependent variable and each independent variable should be linear.

Related procedures. If you believe that none of your predictor variables is correlated with the errors in your dependent variable, you can use the Linear Regression procedure. If your data appear to violate one of the assumptions (such as normality or constant variance), try transforming them. If your data are not related linearly and a transformation does not help, use an alternate model in the Curve Estimation procedure. If your dependent variable is dichotomous, such as whether a particular sale is completed or not, use the Logistic Regression procedure. If your data are not independent—for example, if you observe the same person under several conditions—use the Repeated Measures procedure, available in the SPSS Advanced Models option.

To Obtain a Two-Stage Least-Squares Regression Analysis

▶ From the menus choose:

Analyze
 Regression
  2-Stage Least Squares...

Figure 7.1   2-Stage Least Squares dialog box

▶ Select one dependent variable.

▶ Select one or more explanatory (predictor) variables.

▶ Select one or more instrumental variables.

Explanatory variables not specified as instrumental are considered endogenous. Normally, all of the exogenous variables in the Explanatory list are also specified as instrumental variables.

Two-Stage Least-Squares Regression Options

Figure 7.2   2-Stage Least Squares Options dialog box

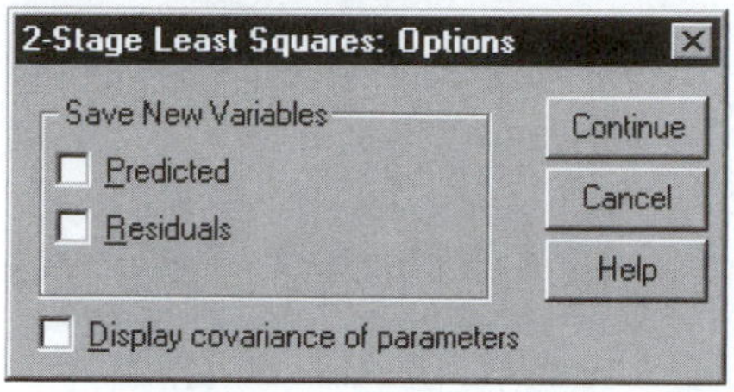

You can select the following options for your analysis:

Save New Variables. Allows you to add new variables to your active file. Available options are Predicted and Residuals.

Display covariance of parameters. Allows you to print the covariance matrix of the parameter estimates.

2SLS Command Additional Features

The SPSS command language also allows you to estimate multiple equations simultaneously.

8 Logistic Regression Analysis Examples

Predicting whether an event will or will not occur, as well as identifying the variables useful in making the prediction, is important in most academic disciplines and in the "real" world. Why do some citizens vote and others do not? Why do some people develop coronary heart disease and others do not? Why do some businesses succeed and others fail?

A variety of multivariate statistical techniques can be used to predict a binary dependent variable from a set of independent variables. Multiple regression analysis and discriminant analysis are two related techniques that quickly come to mind. However, these techniques pose difficulties when the dependent variable can have only two values—an event occurring or not occurring.

When the dependent variable can have only two values, the assumptions necessary for hypothesis testing in regression analysis are necessarily violated. For example, it is unreasonable to assume that the distribution of errors is normal. Another difficulty with multiple regression analysis is that predicted values cannot be interpreted as probabilities. They are not constrained to fall in the interval between 0 and 1.

Linear discriminant analysis does allow direct prediction of group membership, but the assumption of multivariate normality of the independent variables, as well as equal variance-covariance matrices in the two groups, is required for the prediction rule to be optimal.

In this chapter, we will consider another multivariate technique for estimating the probability that an event occurs—the **logistic regression model**. This model requires far fewer assumptions than discriminant analysis; and even when the assumptions required for discriminant analysis are satisfied, logistic regression still performs well. (See Hosmer and Lemeshow, 1989, for an introduction to logistic regression.)

The Logistic Regression Model

In logistic regression, you directly estimate the probability of an event occurring. For the case of a single independent variable, the logistic regression model can be written as

$$\text{Prob (event)} = \frac{e^{B_0 + B_1 X}}{1 + e^{B_0 + B_1 X}}$$

Equation 8.1

or equivalently

$$\text{Prob (event)} = \frac{1}{1 + e^{-(B_0 + B_1 X)}}$$

Equation 8.2

where B_0 and B_1 are coefficients estimated from the data, X is the independent variable, and e is the base of the natural logarithms, approximately 2.718.

For more than one independent variable, the model can be written as

$$\text{Prob (event)} = \frac{e^Z}{1 + e^Z}$$

Equation 8.3

or equivalently

$$\text{Prob (event)} = \frac{1}{1 + e^{-Z}}$$

Equation 8.4

where Z is the linear combination

$$Z = B_0 + B_1 X_1 + B_2 X_2 + ... + B_p X_p$$

Equation 8.5

The probability of the event not occurring is estimated as

$$\text{Prob(no event)} = 1 - \text{Prob(event)}$$

Equation 8.6

Figure 8.1 is a plot of a logistic regression curve when the values of Z are between -5 and $+5$. As you can see, the curve is S-shaped. It closely resembles the curve obtained when the cumulative probability of the normal distribution is plotted. The relationship between the independent variable and the probability is nonlinear. The probability estimates will always be between 0 and 1, regardless of the value of Z.

Figure 8.1   Plot of logistic regression curve

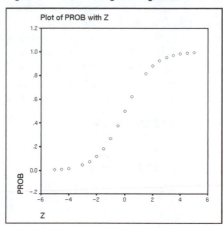

In linear regression, we estimate the parameters of the model using the **least-squares method**. That is, we select regression coefficients that result in the smallest sums of squared distances between the observed and the predicted values of the dependent variable.

In logistic regression, the parameters of the model are estimated using the **maximum-likelihood method**. That is, the coefficients that make our observed results most likely are selected. Since the logistic regression model is nonlinear, an iterative algorithm is necessary for parameter estimation.

An Example

The treatment and prognosis of cancer depends on how much the disease has spread. One of the regions to which a cancer may spread is the lymph nodes. If the lymph nodes are involved, the prognosis is generally poorer than if they are not. That's why it's desirable to establish as early as possible whether the lymph nodes are cancerous. For certain cancers, exploratory surgery is done just to determine whether the nodes are cancerous, since this will determine what treatment is needed. If we could predict whether the nodes are affected or not on the basis of data that can be obtained without performing surgery, considerable discomfort and expense could be avoided.

For this chapter, we will use data presented by Brown (1980) for 53 men with prostate cancer. For each patient, he reports the age, serum acid phosphatase (a laboratory value that is elevated if the tumor has spread to certain areas), the stage of the disease (an indication of how advanced the disease is), the grade of the tumor (an indication of aggressiveness), and X-ray results, as well as whether the cancer had spread to the regional lymph nodes at the time of surgery. The problem is to predict whether the nodes are positive for cancer based on the values of the variables that can be measured without surgery.

Coefficients for the Logistic Model

Figure 8.2 contains the estimated coefficients (under column heading *B*) and related statistics from the logistic regression model that predicts nodal involvement from a constant and the variables *age*, *acid*, *xray*, *stage*, and *grade*. The last three of these variables (*xray*, *stage*, and *grade*) are **indicator variables**, coded 0 or 1. The value of 1 for *xray* indicates positive X-ray findings, the value of 1 for *stage* indicates advanced stage, and the value of 1 for *grade* indicates a more aggressively spreading malignant tumor.

Figure 8.2   Parameter estimates for the logistic regression model

```
----------------- Variables in the Equation ------------------

Variable            B        S.E.      Wald     df      Sig        R

ACID             .0243      .0132    3.4229      1     .0643     .1423
AGE             -.0693      .0579    1.4320      1     .2314     .0000
XRAY            2.0453      .8072    6.4207      1     .0113     .2509
GRADE            .7614      .7708     .9758      1     .3232     .0000
STAGE           1.5641      .7740    4.0835      1     .0433     .1722
Constant         .0618     3.4599     .0003      1     .9857
```

```
                              95% CI for Exp(B)
Variable         Exp(B)      Lower      Upper

ACID             1.0246      .9986     1.0514
AGE               .9331      .8330     1.0452
XRAY             7.7317     1.5893    37.6136
GRADE            2.1413      .4727     9.6996
STAGE            4.7783     1.0482    21.7825
```

Given these coefficients, the logistic regression equation for the probability of nodal involvement can be written as

$$\text{Prob (nodal involvement)} = \frac{1}{1 + e^{-Z}}$$

Equation 8.7

where

$$Z = 0.0618 - 0.0693(\text{age}) + 0.0243(\text{acid}) + 2.0453(\text{xray})$$
$$+ 0.7614(\text{grade}) + 1.5641(\text{stage})$$

Equation 8.8

Applying this to a man who is 66 years old, with a serum acid phosphatase level of 48 and values of 0 for the remaining independent variables, we find

$$Z = 0.0618 - 0.0693(66) + 0.0243(48) = -3.346$$

Equation 8.9

The probability of nodal involvement is then estimated to be

$$\text{Prob (nodal involvement)} = \frac{1}{1 + e^{-(-3.346)}} = 0.0340 \qquad \textbf{Equation 8.10}$$

Based on this estimate, we would predict that the nodes are unlikely to be malignant. In general, if the estimated probability of the event is less than 0.5, we predict that the event will not occur. If the probability is greater than 0.5, we predict that the event will occur. (In the unlikely event that the probability is exactly 0.5, we can flip a coin for our prediction.)

Testing Hypotheses about the Coefficients

For large sample sizes, the test that a coefficient is 0 can be based on the **Wald statistic**, which has a chi-square distribution. When a variable has a single degree of freedom, the Wald statistic is just the square of the ratio of the coefficient to its standard error. For categorical variables, the Wald statistic has degrees of freedom equal to one less than the number of categories.

For example, the coefficient for age is -0.0693, and its standard error is 0.0579. (The standard errors for the logistic regression coefficients are shown in the column labeled *S.E.* in Figure 8.2.) The Wald statistic is $(-0.0693/0.0579)^2$, or about 1.432. The significance level for the Wald statistic is shown in the column labeled *Sig.* In this example, only the coefficients for *xray* and *stage* appear to be significantly different from 0, using a significance level of 0.05.

Unfortunately, the Wald statistic has a very undesirable property. When the absolute value of the regression coefficient becomes large, the estimated standard error is too large. This produces a Wald statistic that is too small, leading you to fail to reject the null hypothesis that the coefficient is 0, when in fact you should. Therefore, whenever you have a large coefficient, you should not rely on the Wald statistic for hypothesis testing. Instead, you should build a model with and without that variable and base your hypothesis test on the change in the log-likelihood (Hauck and Donner, 1977).

Partial Correlation

As is the case with multiple regression, the contribution of individual variables in logistic regression is difficult to determine. The contribution of each variable depends on the other variables in the model. This is a problem, particularly when independent variables are highly correlated.

A statistic that is used to look at the partial correlation between the dependent variable and each of the independent variables is the *R* statistic, shown in Figure 8.2. *R* can range in value from -1 to $+1$. A positive value indicates that as the variable increases in value, so does the likelihood of the event occurring. If *R* is negative, the opposite is true. Small values for R indicate that the variable has a small partial contribution to the model.

The equation for the R statistic is

$$R = \pm \sqrt{\left(\frac{\text{Wald statistic} - 2K}{-2LL_{(0)}} \right)}$$

Equation 8.11

where K is the degrees of freedom for the variable (Atkinson, 1980). The denominator is -2 times the log-likelihood of a base model that contains only the intercept, or a model with no variables if there is no intercept. (If you enter several blocks of variables, the base model for each block is the result of previous entry steps.) The sign of the corresponding coefficient is attached to R. The value of $2K$ in Equation 8.11 is an adjustment for the number of parameters estimated. If the Wald statistic is less than $2K$, R is set to 0.

Interpreting the Regression Coefficients

In multiple linear regression, the interpretation of the regression coefficient is straightforward. It tells you the amount of change in the dependent variable for a one-unit change in the independent variable.

To understand the interpretation of the logistic coefficients, consider a rearrangement of the equation for the logistic model. The logistic model can be rewritten in terms of the odds of an event occurring. (The **odds** of an event occurring are defined as the ratio of the probability that it will occur to the probability that it will not. For example, the odds of getting a head on a single flip of a coin are $0.5/0.5 = 1$. Similarly, the odds of getting a diamond on a single draw from a card deck are $0.25/0.75 = 1/3$. Don't confuse this technical meaning of odds with its informal usage to mean simply the probability.)

First let's write the logistic model in terms of the log of the odds, which is called a **logit**:

$$\log\left(\frac{\text{Prob(event)}}{\text{Prob(no event)}} \right) = B_0 + B_1 X_1 + \ldots + B_p X_p$$

Equation 8.12

From Equation 8.12, you see that the logistic coefficient can be interpreted as the change in the log odds associated with a one-unit change in the independent variable. For example, from Figure 8.2, you see that the coefficient for *grade* is 0.76. This tells you that when the grade changes from 0 to 1 and the values of the other independent variables remain the same, the log odds of the nodes being malignant increase by 0.76.

Since it's easier to think of odds rather than log odds, the logistic equation can be written in terms of odds as

$$\frac{\text{Prob (event)}}{\text{Prob (no event)}} = e^{B_0 + B_1 X_1 + \ldots + B_p X_p} = e^{B_0} e^{B_1 X_1} \ldots e^{B_p X_p}$$

Equation 8.13

Then e raised to the power B_i is the factor by which the odds change when the ith independent variable increases by one unit. If B_i is positive, this factor will be greater than 1, which means that the odds are increased; if B_i is negative, the factor will be less than 1, which means that the odds are decreased. When B_i is 0, the factor equals 1, which leaves the odds unchanged. For example, when *grade* changes from 0 to 1, the odds are increased by a factor of 2.14, as is shown in the *Exp(B)* column in Figure 8.2.

As a further example, let's calculate the odds of having malignant nodes for a 60-year-old man with a serum acid phosphatase level of 62, a value of 1 for X-ray results, and values of 0 for stage and grade of tumor. First, calculate the probability that the nodes are malignant:

$$\text{Estimated prob (malignant nodes)} = \frac{1}{1 + e^{-Z}}$$

Equation 8.14

where

$$Z = 0.0618 - 0.0693(60) + 0.0243(62) + 2.0453(1)$$
$$+ 0.7614(0) + (1.5641)(0) = -0.54$$

Equation 8.15

The estimated probability of malignant nodes is therefore 0.37. The probability of not having malignant nodes is 0.63 (that is, $1 - 0.37$). The *odds* of having a malignant node are then estimated as

$$\text{Odds} = \frac{\text{Prob (event)}}{\text{Prob (no event)}} = \frac{0.37}{1 - 0.37} = 0.59$$

Equation 8.16

and the log odds are -0.53.

What would be the probability of malignant nodes if, instead of 0, the case had a value of 1 for *grade*? Following the same procedure as before, but using a value of 1 for *grade*, the estimated probability of malignant nodes is 0.554. Similarly, the estimated odds are 1.24, and the log odds are 0.22.

By increasing the value of *grade* by one unit, we have increased the log odds by about 0.75, the value of the coefficient for *grade*. (Since we didn't use many digits in our hand calculations, our value of 0.75 isn't exactly equal to the 0.76 value for *grade* shown in Figure 8.2. If we carried the computations out with enough precision, we would arrive at exactly the value of the coefficient.)

By increasing the value of *grade* from 0 to 1, the odds changed from 0.59 to 1.24. The ratio of the odds of positive nodes when *grade* is 1 to the same odds when *grade* is 0 is about 2.1. This ratio is called the **odds ratio**. The odds ratio for a variable tells you change in odds for a case when the value of that variable increases by 1. The odds ratio for *grade* is in the column labeled *Exp(B)* in Figure 8.2. Its 95% confidence interval is in the last two columns (the second part) of Figure 8.2. From the 95% confidence interval, you can see that values anywhere from 0.47 to 9.7 are plausible for the population value of the odds ratio for *grade*. Since this interval includes the value 1—no change in odds—you can't conclude based on this sample of data that a unit change in *grade* in the population is associated with a change in the odds of positive nodes. (Since the confidence interval for the odds ratio is based on the confidence interval for the corresponding logistic regression coefficient, the confidence interval for the odds ratio will include 1 whenever the confidence interval for the regression coefficient contains 0.)

When an independent variable is continuous, such as age, blood pressure, or years of education, the odds ratio for a unit change in the value of the independent variable may be less informative than the odds ratio associated with a decade change in age, or a 5 mm change in blood pressure.

Assessing the Goodness of Fit of the Model

Whenever you fit a model to data, you want to know how well the model fits not only the sample of data from which it is derived, but also the population from which the sample data were selected. A model always fits the sample you used to estimate it better than it will fit the population. For large data sets, it may be feasible to split the data into two parts. You can estimate a model on one part and then apply the model to the other to see how well it fits. There are also other statistical techniques with picturesque names such as "jackknifing" and "bootstrapping" that are useful for assessing how well the model would fit another set of data.

Two additional criteria for evaluating model performance in logistic regression are called model discrimination and model calibration. **Model discrimination** evaluates the ability of the model to distinguish between the two groups of cases, based on the estimated probability of the event occurring. That is, you want to know how well the predicted probabilities of the event occurring separate the cases for whom the outcome actually occurs and those for whom it does not. **Model calibration** evaluates how well the observed and predicted probabilities agree over the entire range of probability values. Let's first consider some simple ways to examine model discrimination. "Another Look at Model Fit" on p. 59 continues this topic by presenting summary measures of model discrimination and calibration.

The Classification Table

One way to assess how well our model fits is to compare our predictions to the observed outcomes. Figure 8.3 compares the observed and predicted group memberships when cases with a predicted probability of 0.5 or greater are classified as having positive nodes.

Figure 8.3   Classification table

```
Classification Table for NODES
The Cut Value is .50
                    Predicted
                 Neg      Pos      Percent Correct
                  N  I     P
Observed        +-------+-------+
  Neg     N    I   28  I    5  I    84.85%
                +-------+-------+
  Pos     P    I    7  I   13  I    65.00%
                +-------+-------+
                         Overall   77.36%
```

From the table, you see that 28 patients without malignant nodes were correctly predicted by the model not to have malignant nodes. Similarly, 13 men with positive nodes were correctly predicted to have positive nodes. The off-diagonal entries of the table tell you how many men were incorrectly classified. A total of 12 men were misclassified in this example—5 men with negative nodes and 7 men with positive nodes. Of the men without diseased nodes, 84.85% were correctly classified. Of the men with diseased nodes, 65% were correctly classified. Overall, 77.36% of the 53 men were correctly classified.

The classification table doesn't reveal the distribution of estimated probabilities for men in the two groups. For each predicted group, the table shows only whether the estimated probability is greater or less than one-half. For example, you cannot tell from the table whether the seven patients who had false negative results had predicted probabilities near 50%, or low predicted probabilities. Ideally, you would like the two groups to have very different estimated probabilities. That is, you would like to see small estimated probabilities of positive nodes for all men without malignant nodes and large estimated probabilities for all men with malignant nodes.

Histogram of Estimated Probabilities

Figure 8.4 is a histogram of the estimated probabilities of cancerous nodes. The symbol used for each case designates the group to which the case actually belongs. If you have a model that successfully distinguishes the two groups, the cases for which the event has occurred should be to the right of 0.5, while the cases for which the event has not occurred should be to the left of 0.5. The more the two groups cluster at their respective ends of the plot, the better.

Figure 8.4   Histogram of estimated probabilities

```
             Observed Groups and Predicted Probabilities

        4 +   NN                                                          +
          I   NN                                                          I
          I   NN                                                          I
   F      I   NN                                                          I
   R    3 +   NN     P            P                            P          +
   E      I   NN     P            P                            P          I
   Q      I   NN     P            P                            P          I
   U      I   NN     P            P                            P          I
   E    2 +   NNNN   N   PP       N       P    PP              P    P     +
   N      I   NNNN   N   PP       N       P    PP              P    P     I
   C      I   NNNN   N   PP       N       P    PP              P    P     I
   Y      I   NNNN   N   PP       N       P    PP              P    P     I
        1 +   NNNNNNNPNNNN NNPNN   N    NN NNN N    P P  P P P NP PP       +
          I   NNNNNNNPNNNN NNPNN   N    NN NNN N    P P  P P P NP PP       I
          I   NNNNNNNPNNNN NNPNN   N    NN NNN N    P P  P P P NP PP       I
          I   NNNNNNNPNNNN NNPNN   N    NN NNN N    P P  P P P NP PP       I
Predicted -------------+-------------+-------------+---------------
   Prob:  0             .25          .5           .75             1
   Group: NNNNNNNNNNNNNNNNNNNNNNNNNNNNNNNNNNNNNNNPPPPPPPPPPPPPPPPPPPPPPPPPPPPPPP

             Predicted Probability is of Membership for Pos
             The Cut Value is .50
             Symbols: N - Neg
                      P - Pos
             Each Symbol Represents .25 Cases.
```

From Figure 8.4, you see that there is only one noncancerous case with a high estimated probability of having positive nodes (the case identified with the letter *N* at a probability value of about 0.88). However, there are four diseased cases with estimated probabilities less than 0.25.

By looking at this histogram of predicted probabilities, you can see whether a different rule for assigning cases to groups might be useful. For example, if most of the misclassifications occur in the region around 0.5, you might decide to withhold judgment for cases with values in this region. In this example, this means that you would predict nodal involvement only for cases where you were reasonably sure that the logistic prediction would be correct. You might decide to operate on all questionable cases.

If the consequences of misclassification are not the same in both directions (for example, calling nodes negative when they are really positive is worse than calling nodes positive when they are really negative), the classification rule can be altered to decrease the possibility of making the more severe error. For example, you might decide to call cases "negative" only if their estimated probability is less than 0.3. By looking at the histogram of the estimated probabilities, you can get some idea of how different classification rules might perform. (Of course, when you apply the model to new cases, you can't expect the classification rule to behave exactly the same.)

Goodness of Fit of the Model

Seeing how well the model classifies the observed data is one way of determining how well the logistic model performs. Another way of assessing the goodness of fit of the model is to examine how "likely" the sample results actually are, given the parameter estimates. (Recall that we chose parameter estimates that would make our observed results as likely as possible.)

The probability of the observed results, given the parameter estimates, is known as the **likelihood**. Since the likelihood is a small number less than 1, it is customary to use -2 times the log of the likelihood ($-2LL$) as a measure of how well the estimated model fits the data. A good model is one that results in a high likelihood of the observed results. This translates to a small value for $-2LL$. (If a model fits perfectly, the likelihood is 1, and -2 times the log-likelihood is 0.)

For the logistic regression model that contains only the constant, $-2LL$ is 70.25, as shown in Figure 8.5.

Figure 8.5 $-2LL$ for model containing only the constant

```
Dependent Variable..   NODES

Beginning Block Number  0.   Initial Log Likelihood Function

-2 Log Likelihood   70.252153

* Constant is included in the model.

No terms in the model.
```

Another measure of how well the model fits is the **goodness-of-fit statistic**, which compares the observed probabilities to those predicted by the model. The goodness-of-fit statistic is defined as

$$Z^2 = \sum \frac{\text{Residual}_i^2}{P_i(1 - P_i)}$$

Equation 8.17

where the residual is the difference between the observed value, Y_i, and the predicted value, P_i.

Goodness of Fit with All Variables

Figure 8.6 shows the goodness-of-fit statistics for the model with all of the independent variables. For the current model, the value of $-2LL$ is 48.126, which is smaller than the $-2LL$ for the model containing only a constant. The goodness-of-fit statistic is displayed in the second row of the table. The next two entries, the *Cox & Snell R^2* and the *Nagelkerke R^2*, are statistics that attempt to quantify the proportion of explained "variation" in the logistic regression model. They are similar in intent to the R^2 in a linear regression model, although the variation in a logistic regression model must be defined differently.

The Cox and Snell R^2 is

$$R^2 = 1 - \left[\frac{L(0)}{L(B)}\right]^{2/N}$$ **Equation 8.18**

where $L(0)$ is the likelihood for the model with only a constant, $L(B)$ is the likelihood for the model under consideration, and N is the sample size. The problem with this measure for logistic regression is that it cannot achieve a maximum value of 1. Nagelkerke (1991) proposed a modification of the Cox and Snell R^2 so that the value of 1 could be achieved. The Nagelkerke $\tilde{R}^2$ is

$$\tilde{R}^2 = \frac{R^2}{R^2{}_{MAX}}$$ **Equation 8.19**

where $R^2{}_{MAX} = 1 - [L(0)]^{2/N}$

From the Nagelkerke $\tilde{R}^2$, you can see that about 47% of the "variation" in the outcome variable is explained by the logistic regression model.

Figure 8.6   Statistics for model containing the independent variables

```
-2 Log Likelihood        48.126
Goodness of Fit          46.790
Cox & Snell - R2           .341
Nagelkerke - R2            .465
```

	Chi-Square	df	Significance
Model	22.126	5	.0005
Block	22.126	5	.0005
Step	22.126	5	.0005

There are three additional chi-square entries in Figure 8.6. They are labeled *Model, Block,* and *Step.* The model chi-square is the difference between $-2LL$ for the model with only a constant and $-2LL$ for the current model. (If a constant is not included in the model, the likelihood for the model without any variables is used for comparison.) Thus, the model chi-square tests the null hypothesis that the coefficients for all of the terms in the current model, except the constant, are 0. This is comparable to the overall F test for regression.

In this example, $-2LL$ for the model containing only the constant is 70.252 (from Figure 8.5), while for the complete model, it is 48.126. The model chi-square, 22.126, is the difference between these two values. The degrees of freedom for the model chi-square is the difference between the number of parameters in the two models.

The entry labeled *Block* is the change in $-2LL$ between successive entry blocks during model building (see "To Obtain a Logistic Regression Analysis" on p. 4 for information on entering variables in blocks). In this example, we entered our variables in a single block, so the block chi-square is the same as the model chi-square. If you enter variables in more than one block, these chi-square values will be different.

The entry labeled *Step* is the change in $-2LL$ between successive steps of building a model. It tests the null hypothesis that the coefficients for the variables added at the last step are 0. In this example, we considered only two models: the constant-only model and the model with a constant and five independent variables. Thus, the model chi-square, the block chi-square, and the step chi-square values are all the same. If you sequentially consider more than just these two models, using either forward or backward variable selection, the block chi-square and step chi-square will differ. The step chi-square test is comparable to the F-change test in stepwise multiple regression.

Categorical Variables

In logistic regression, just as in linear regression, the codes for the independent variables must be meaningful. You cannot take a nominal variable, such as religion, assign arbitrary codes from 1 to 35, and then use the resulting variable in the model. In this situation, you must recode the values of the independent variable by creating a new set of variables that correspond in some way to the original categories.

If you have a two-category variable, such as sex, you can code each case as 0 or 1 to indicate either female or not female. Or, you could code it as being male or not male. This is called **dummy-variable** or **indicator-variable coding**. *Grade*, *stage*, and *xray* are all examples of two-category variables that have been coded as 0 and 1. The code of 1 indicates that the poorer outcome is present. The interpretation of the resulting coefficients for *grade*, *stage*, and *xray* is straightforward. It tells you the difference between the log odds when a case is a member of the "poor" category and when it is not.

When you have a variable with more than two categories, you must create new variables to represent the categories. The number of new variables required to represent a categorical variable is one less than the number of categories. For example, if instead of the actual values for serum acid phosphatase, you had values of 1, 2, or 3, depending on whether the value was low, medium, or high, you would have to create two new variables to represent the serum phosphatase effect. Two alternative coding schemes are described in "Indicator-Variable Coding Scheme" below and "Another Coding Scheme" on p. 49.

Indicator-Variable Coding Scheme

One of the ways you can create two new variables for serum acid phosphatase is to use indicator variables to represent the categories. With this method, one variable would represent the low value, coded 1 if the value is low and 0 otherwise. The second variable would represent the medium value, coded 1 if the value is average and 0 otherwise. The value "high" would be represented by codes of 0 for both of these variables. The choice of the category to be coded as 0 for both variables is arbitrary.

With categorical variables, the only statement you can make about the effect of a particular category is in comparison to some other category. For example, if you have a variable that represents type of cancer, you can only make statements such as "lung cancer compared to bladder cancer decreases your chance of survival." Or you might say that "lung cancer compared to all the cancer types in the study decreases your chance of survival." You can't make a statement about lung cancer without relating it to the other types of cancer.

If you use indicator variables for coding, the coefficients for the new variables represent the effect of each category compared to a reference category. The coefficient for the reference category is 0. As an example, consider Figure 8.7. The variable *catacid1* is the indicator variable for low serum acid phosphatase, coded 1 for low levels and 0 otherwise. Similarly, the variable *catacid2* is the indicator variable for medium serum acid phosphatase. The reference category is high levels.

Figure 8.7   Indicator variables

```
--------------------- Variables in the Equation ----------------------

Variable          B        S.E.     Wald     df     Sig        R      Exp(B)

AGE            -.0522      .0630    .6862      1    .4075     .0000     .9492
CATACID1      -2.0079     1.0520   3.6427      1    .0563    -.1529     .1343
CATACID2      -1.0923      .9264   1.3903      1    .2384     .0000     .3355
XRAY           2.0348      .8375   5.9033      1    .0151     .2357    7.6503
GRADE           .8076      .8233    .9623      1    .3266     .0000    2.2426
STAGE          1.4571      .7683   3.5968      1    .0579     .1508    4.2934
Constant       1.7698     3.8088    .2159      1    .6422
```

The coefficient for *catacid1* is the change in log odds when you have a low value compared to a high value. Similarly, *catacid2* is the change in log odds when you have a medium value compared to a high value. The coefficient for the high value is necessarily 0, since it does not differ from itself. In Figure 8.7, you see that the coefficients for both of the indicator variables are negative. This means that compared to high values for serum acid phosphatase, low and medium values are associated with decreased log odds of malignant nodes. The low category decreases the log odds more than the medium category.

The SPSS Logistic Regression procedure will automatically create new variables for variables declared as categorical (see "Logistic Regression Define Categorical Variables" on p. 5 in Chapter 2). You can choose the coding scheme you want to use for the new variables.

Figure 8.8 shows the table that is displayed for each categorical variable. The rows of the table correspond to the categories of the variable. The actual value is given in the column labeled *Value*. The number of cases with each value is displayed in the column labeled *Freq*. Subsequent columns correspond to new variables created by the program. The number in parentheses indicates the suffix used to identify the variable in the output.

The codes that represent each original category using the new variables are listed under the corresponding new-variable column.

Figure 8.8   Indicator-variable coding scheme

```
                               Parameter
                  Value   Freq  Coding
                                (1)    (2)
CATACID
                  1.00    15    1.000   .000
                  2.00    20     .000  1.000
                  3.00    18     .000   .000
```

From Figure 8.8, you see that there are 20 cases with a value of 2 for *catacid*. Each of these cases will be assigned a code of 0 for the new variable *catacid(1)* and a code of 1 for the new variable *catacid(2)*. Similarly, cases with a value of 3 for *catacid* will be given the code of 0 for both *catacid(1)* and *catacid(2)*.

Another Coding Scheme

The statement you can make based on the logistic regression coefficients depends on how you have created the new variables used to represent the categorical variable. As shown in the previous section, when you use indicator variables for coding, the coefficients for the new variables represent the effect of each category compared to a reference category. If, on the other hand, you wanted to compare the effect of each category to the average effect of all of the categories, you could have selected the deviation coding scheme shown in Figure 8.9. This differs from indicator-variable coding only in that the last category is coded as −1 for each of the new variables.

With this coding scheme, the logistic regression coefficients tell you how much better or worse each category is compared to the average effect of all categories, as shown in Figure 8.10. For each new variable, the coefficients now represent the difference from the average effect over all categories. The value of the coefficient for the last category is not displayed, but it is no longer 0. Instead, it is the negative of the sum of the displayed coefficients. From Figure 8.10, the coefficient for "high" level is calculated as $-(-0.9745 - 0.0589) = 1.0334$.

Figure 8.9   Another coding scheme

```
                               Parameter
                  Value   Freq  Coding
                                (1)     (2)
CATACID
                  1.00    15    1.000    .000
                  2.00    20     .000   1.000
                  3.00    18   -1.000  -1.000
```

Note that the parameter coding shown in Figure 8.9 tells you how the data values are transformed to obtain the specified type of parameter estimates. The parameter coding table shows you the linear combination of categories corresponding to each parameter estimate only if the contrasts that you specify are orthogonal. Since deviation contrasts are not orthogonal, the parameter coding shown in Figure 8.9 does not tell you what levels of a categorical variable are being compared. It tells you how the categorical variable is being transformed so that deviation contrasts for the parameter estimates are obtained. The appendix provides detailed information about all of the available contrasts.

Figure 8.10   New coefficients

```
---------------------- Variables in the Equation -----------------------

Variable            B      S.E.     Wald    df     Sig       R    Exp(B)

AGE             -.0522    .0630    .6862    1    .4075    .0000    .9492
CATACID                            3.8361   2    .1469    .0000
 CATACID(1)     -.9745    .6410    2.3116   1    .1284   -.0666    .3774
 CATACID(2)     -.0589    .5727    .0106    1    .9181    .0000    .9428
XRAY            2.0348    .8375    5.9033   1    .0151    .2357   7.6503
GRADE            .8076    .8233    .9623    1    .3266    .0000   2.2426
STAGE           1.4571    .7683    3.5968   1    .0579    .1508   4.2934
Constant         .7364   3.7352    .0389    1    .8437
```

Different coding schemes result in different logistic regression coefficients, but not in different conclusions. That is, even though the actual values of the coefficients differ between Figure 8.7 and Figure 8.10, they tell you the same thing. Figure 8.7 tells you the effect of category 1 compared to category 3, while Figure 8.10 tells you the effect of category 1 compared to the average effect of all of the categories. You can select the coding scheme to match the type of comparisons you want to make.

Interaction Terms

Just as in linear regression, you can include terms in the model that are products of single terms. For example, if it made sense, you could include a term for the *acid* by *age* interaction in your model.

Interaction terms for categorical variables can also be computed. They are created as products of the values of the new variables. For categorical variables, make sure that the interaction terms created are those of interest. If you are using categorical variables with indicator coding, the interaction terms generated as the product of the variables are generally not those that you are interested in. Consider, for example, the interaction term between two indicator variables. If you just multiply the variables together, you will obtain a value of 1 only if both of the variables are coded "present." What you would probably like is a code of 1 if both of the variables are present or both are absent.

Selecting Predictor Variables

In logistic regression, as in other multivariate statistical techniques, you may want to identify subsets of independent variables that are good predictors of the dependent variable. All of the problems associated with variable selection algorithms in regression and discriminant analysis are found in logistic regression as well. None of the algorithms result in a "best" model in any statistical sense. Different algorithms for variable selection may result in different models. It is a good idea to examine several possible models and choose from among them on the basis of interpretability, parsimony, and ease of variable acquisition.

As always, the model is selected to fit a particular sample well, so there is no assurance that the same model will be selected if another sample from the same population is taken. The model will always fit the sample better than the population from which it is selected.

The SPSS Logistic Regression procedure has several methods available for model selection. You can enter variables into the model at will. You can also use forward stepwise selection and backward stepwise elimination for automated model building. The score statistic is always used for entering variables into a model. The Wald statistic, the change in likelihood, or the conditional statistic can be used for removing variables from a model (Lawless and Singhal, 1978). All variables that are used to represent the same categorical variable are entered or removed from the model together.

Forward Stepwise Selection

Forward stepwise variable selection in logistic regression proceeds the same way as in multiple linear regression. You start out with a model that contains only the constant unless the option to omit the constant term from the model is selected. At each step, the variable with the smallest significance level for the score statistic, provided it is less than the chosen cutoff value (by default 0.05), is entered into the model. All variables in the forward stepwise block that have been entered are then examined to see if they meet removal criteria. If the Wald statistic is used for deleting variables, the Wald statistics for all variables in the model are examined and the variable with the largest significance level for the Wald statistic, provided it exceeds the chosen cutoff value (by default 0.1), is removed from the model. If no variables meet removal criteria, the next eligible variable is entered into the model.

If a variable is selected for removal and it results in a model that has already been considered, variable selection stops. Otherwise, the model is estimated without the deleted variable and the variables are again examined for removal. This continues until no more variables are eligible for removal. Then variables are again examined for entry into the model. The process continues until either a previously considered model is encountered (which means the algorithm is cycling) or no variables meet entry or removal criteria.

The Likelihood-Ratio Test

A better criterion than the Wald statistic for determining variables to be removed from the model is the **likelihood-ratio (LR) test**. This involves estimating the model with each variable eliminated in turn and looking at the change in the log-likelihood when each variable is deleted. The likelihood-ratio test for the null hypothesis that the coefficients of the terms removed are 0 is obtained by dividing the likelihood for the reduced model by the likelihood for the full model.

If the null hypothesis is true and the sample size is sufficiently large, the quantity −2 times the log of the likelihood-ratio statistic has a chi-square distribution with r degrees of freedom, where r is the difference between the number of terms in the full model and the reduced model. (The model chi-square and the improvement chi-square are both likelihood-ratio tests.)

When the likelihood-ratio test is used for removing terms from a model, its significance level is compared to the cutoff value. The algorithm proceeds as previously described but with the likelihood-ratio statistic, instead of the Wald statistic, being evaluated for removing variables.

You can also use the **conditional statistic** to test for removal. Like the likelihood-ratio test, the conditional statistic is based on the difference in the likelihood for the reduced and full models. However, the conditional statistic is computationally much less intensive since it does not require that the model be reestimated without each of the variables.

An Example of Forward Selection

To see what the output looks like for forward selection, consider Figure 8.11, which contains part of the summary statistics for the model when the constant is the only term included. First you see the previously described statistics for the constant. Then you see statistics for variables not in the equation. (The R for variables not in the equation is calculated using the score statistic instead of the Wald statistic.)

Figure 8.11   Variables not in the equation

```
--------------------- Variables in the Equation ----------------------

Variable           B        S.E.     Wald     df      Sig       R     Exp(B)

Constant        -.5008     .2834    3.1227     1     .0772

-------------- Variables not in the Equation ----------------
Residual Chi Square        19.451 with        5 df      Sig =   .0016

Variable           Score     df      Sig        R

AGE               1.0945      1     .2955     .0000
ACID              3.1168      1     .0775     .1261
XRAY             11.2829      1     .0008     .3635
STAGE             7.4381      1     .0064     .2782
GRADE             4.0745      1     .0435     .1718
```

The residual chi-square statistic tests the null hypothesis that the coefficients for all variables not in the model are 0. (The residual chi-square statistic is calculated from the score statistics, so it is not exactly the same value as the improvement chi-square value that you see in Figure 8.6. In general, however, the two statistics should be similar in value.) If the observed significance level for the residual chi-square statistic is small (that is, if you have reason to reject the hypothesis that all of the coefficients are 0), it is sensible to proceed with variable selection. If you can't reject the hypothesis that the coefficients are 0, you should consider terminating variable selection. If you continue to build a model, there is a reasonable chance that your resulting model will not be useful for other samples from the same population.

In this example, the significance level for the residual chi-square is small, so we can proceed with variable selection. For each variable not in the model, the score statistic and its significance level, if the variable were entered next into the model, is shown. The score statistic is an efficient alternative to the Wald statistic for testing the hypothesis that a coefficient is 0. Unlike the Wald statistic, it does not require the explicit computation of parameter estimates, so it is useful in situations where recalculating parameter estimates for many different models would be computationally prohibitive. The likelihood-ratio statistic, the Wald statistic, and Rao's efficient score statistic are all equivalent in large samples, when the null hypothesis is true (Rao, 1973).

From Figure 8.11, you see that *xray* has the smallest observed significance level less than 0.05, the default value for entry, so it is entered into the model. Statistics for variables not in the model at this step are shown in Figure 8.12. You see that the *stage* variable has the smallest observed significance level and meets entry criteria, so it is entered next. Figure 8.13 contains logistic coefficients when *stage* is included in the model. Since the observed significance levels of the coefficients for both variables in the model are less than 0.1, the default criterion for removal, neither variable is removed from the model.

Figure 8.12   Variables not in the equation

```
--------------- Variables not in the Equation ----------------
Residual Chi Square       10.360 with       4 df    Sig =  .0348

Variable          Score      df      Sig       R

AGE              1.3524       1     .2449    .0000
ACID             2.0732       1     .1499    .0323
STAGE            5.6393       1     .0176    .2276
GRADE            2.3710       1     .1236    .0727
```

Figure 8.13   Logistic coefficients with variables stage and xray

```
---------------------- Variables in the Equation ----------------------
Variable         B       S.E.      Wald     df      Sig       R      Exp(B)

XRAY          2.1194     .7468    8.0537     1     .0045    .2935    8.3265
STAGE         1.5883     .7000    5.1479     1     .0233    .2117    4.8953
Constant     -2.0446     .6100   11.2360     1     .0008
```

The goodness-of-fit statistics for the model with *xray* and *stage* are shown in Figure 8.14. The model chi-square is the difference between $-2LL$ when only the constant is in the model and $-2LL$ when the constant, *xray*, and *stage* are in the model ($70.25 - 53.35 = 16.90$). The small observed significance level for the model chi-square indicates that you can reject the null hypothesis that the coefficients for *xray* and *stage* are zero. The improvement chi-square is the change in $-2LL$ when *stage* is added to a model containing *xray* and the constant. The small observed significance level indicates that the coefficient for *stage* is not zero. (−2*LL* for the model with only the constant and *xray* is 59.001, so the improvement chi-square is 59.00 − 53.35 = 5.65 .)

Figure 8.14   Goodness-of-fit statistics with variables stage and xray

```
-2 Log Likelihood          53.353
Goodness of Fit            54.018
Cox & Snell - R^2            .273
Nagelkerke - R^2             .372

                    Chi-Square    df Significance

Model                   16.899     2        .0002
Block                   16.899     2        .0002
Step                     5.647     1        .0175
```

The statistics for variables not in the model after *stage* is entered are shown in . All three of the observed significance levels are greater than 0.05, so no additional variables are included in the model.

Figure 8.15   Variables not in the model after variable stage

```
--------------- Variables not in the Equation ----------------
Residual Chi Square        5.422 with      3 df     Sig =  .1434

Variable          Score     df     Sig        R

AGE              1.2678      1    .2602    .0000
ACID             3.0917      1    .0787    .1247
GRADE             .5839      1    .4448    .0000
```

Forward Selection with the Likelihood-Ratio Criterion

If you select the likelihood-ratio statistic for deleting variables, the output will look slightly different from that previously described. For variables in the equation at a particular step, output similar to that shown in Figure 8.16 is produced in addition to the usual coefficients and Wald statistics.

Figure 8.16   Removal statistics

```
----------------- Model if Term Removed ------------------

Term        Log                          Significance
Removed     Likelihood    -2 Log LR   df  of Log LR

XRAY        -31.276        9.199       1       .0024
STAGE       -29.500        5.647       1       .0175
```

For each variable in the model, Figure 8.16 contains the log-likelihood for the model if the variable is removed from the model; −2 log LR, which tests the null hypothesis that the coefficient of the term is 0; and the observed significance level. If the observed significance level is greater than the cutoff value for remaining in the model, the term is removed from the model and the model statistics are recalculated to see if any other variables are eligible for removal.

Backward Elimination

Forward selection starts without any variables in the model. Backward elimination starts with all of the variables in the model. Then, at each step, variables are evaluated for entry and removal. The score statistic is always used for determining whether variables should be added to the model. Just as in forward selection, the Wald statistic, the likelihood-ratio statistic, or the conditional statistic can be used to select variables for removal.

Diagnostic Methods

Whenever you build a statistical model, it is important to examine the adequacy of the resulting model. In linear regression, we look at a variety of residuals, measures of influence, and indicators of collinearity. These are valuable tools for identifying points for which the model does not fit well, points that exert a strong influence on the coefficient estimates, and variables that are highly related to each other.

In logistic regression, there are comparable diagnostics that should be used to look for problems. The SPSS Logistic Regression procedure provides a variety of such statistics.

The **residual** is the difference between the observed probability of the event and the predicted probability of the event based on the model. For example, if we predict the probability of malignant nodes to be 0.80 for a man who has malignant nodes, the residual is $1 - 0.80 = 0.20$.

The **standardized residual** is the residual divided by an estimate of its standard deviation. In this case, it is

$$Z_i = \frac{\text{Residual}_i}{\sqrt{P_i(1 - P_i)}}$$
Equation 8.20

For each case, the standardized residual can also be considered a component of the chi-square goodness-of-fit statistic. If the sample size is large, the standardized residuals should be approximately normally distributed, with a mean of 0 and a standard deviation of 1.

For each case, the **deviance** is computed as

$$-2 \times \log(\text{predicted probability for the observed group})$$
Equation 8.21

The deviance is calculated by taking the square root of the above statistic and attaching a negative sign if the event did not occur for that case. For example, the deviance for a man without malignant nodes and a predicted probability of 0.8 for nonmalignant nodes is

$$\text{Deviance} = -\sqrt{-2\log(0.8)} = -0.668$$
Equation 8.22

Large values for deviance indicate that the model does not fit the case well. For large sample sizes, the deviance is approximately normally distributed.

The **Studentized residual** for a case is the change in the model deviance if the case is excluded. Discrepancies between the deviance and the Studentized residual may identify unusual cases. Normal probability plots of the Studentized residuals may be useful.

The **logit residual** is the residual for the model if it is predicted in the logit scale. That is,

$$\text{Logit residual}_i = \frac{\text{residual}_i}{P_i(1 - P_i)}$$

Equation 8.23

The **leverage** in logistic regression is in many respects analogous to the leverage in least-squares regression. Leverage values are often used for detecting observations that have a large impact on the predicted values. Unlike linear regression, the leverage values in logistic regression depend on both the dependent variable scores and the design matrix. Leverage values are bounded by 0 and 1. Their average value is p/n, where p is the number of estimated parameters in the model, including the constant, and n is the sample size.

Cook's distance is a measure of the influence of a case. It tells you how much deleting a case affects not only the residual for that case, but also the residuals of the remaining cases. Cook's distance (D) depends on the standardized residual for a case, as well as its leverage. It is defined as

$$D_i = \frac{Z_i^2 \times h_i}{(1 - h_i)^2}$$

Equation 8.24

where Z_i is the standardized residual and h_i is the leverage.

Another useful diagnostic measure is the change in the logistic coefficients when a case is deleted from the model, or **DfBeta**. You can compute this change for each coefficient, including the constant. For example, the change in the first coefficient when case i is deleted is

$$\text{DfBeta}(B_1^{(i)}) = B_1 - B_1^{(i)}$$

Equation 8.25

where B_1 is the value of the coefficient when all cases are included and $B_1^{(i)}$ is the value of the coefficient when the ith case is excluded. Large values for change identify observations that should be examined.

Plotting Diagnostics

All of the diagnostic statistics described in this chapter can be saved for further analysis. If you save the values for the diagnostics, you can, when appropriate, obtain normal probability plots using the Examine procedure and plot the diagnostics using the Graph procedure (see the *SPSS Base User's Guide* for more information on these procedures).

Figure 8.17 shows a normal probability plot and a detrended normal probability plot of the deviances. As you can see, the deviances do not appear to be normally distributed. That's because there are cases for which the model just doesn't fit well. In Figure 8.4, you see cases that have high probabilities for being in the incorrect group.

Figure 8.17 Normal probability of the deviances

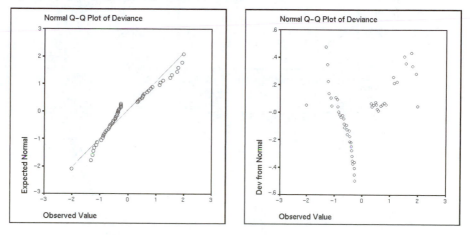

A plot of the standardized residuals against the case sequence numbers is shown in Figure 8.18. Again, you see cases with large values for the standardized residuals. Figure 8.19 shows that there is one case with a leverage value that is much larger than the rest. Similarly, Figure 8.20 shows that there is a case that has substantial impact on the estimation of the coefficient for *acid* (case 24). Examination of the data reveals that this case has the largest value for serum acid phosphatase and yet does not have malignant nodes. Since serum acid phosphatase was positively related to malignant nodes, as shown in Figure 8.2, this case is quite unusual. If we remove case 24 from the analysis, the coefficient for serum acid phosphatase changes from 0.0243 to 0.0490. A variable that was, at best, a very marginal predictor becomes much more important.

Figure 8.18   Plot of standardized residual with case ID

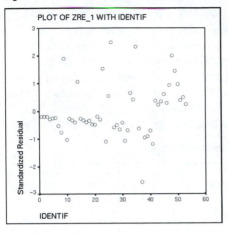

Figure 8.19   Plot of leverage with case ID

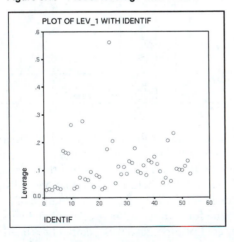

Figure 8.20   Plot of change in acid coefficient with case ID

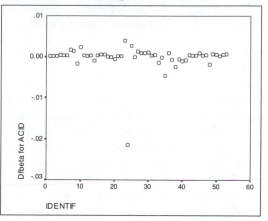

Another Look at Model Fit

Model Discrimination

In "Assessing the Goodness of Fit of the Model" on p. 42, two criteria for model evaluation were introduced: model discrimination and model calibration. Let's first consider model discrimination. Model discrimination tells you how well the model is able to distinguish between cases in the two groups. A perfect model always assigns higher probabilities to cases with the outcome of interest than to cases without the outcome of interest. In other words, the two sets of probabilities do not overlap.

A frequently used measure of the ability of a model to discriminate between the two groups of cases is the c statistic. The **c statistic** can be interpreted as the proportion of pairs of cases with different observed outcomes in which the model results in a higher probability for the cases with the event than for the case without the event. (The c statistic is equal to the area under the ROC curve. For further information, see Hanley and McNeil, 1982.) The c statistic ranges in value from 0.5 to 1. A value of 0.5 means that the model is no better than flipping a coin for assigning cases to groups. A value of 1 means that the model always assigns higher probabilities to cases with the event than to cases without the event.

To calculate the c statistic in SPSS, you must first save the predicted probabilities from logistic regression. Then, using the COMPUTE facility, you must calculate a new variable that groups the predicted probabilities into a large number of distinct groups. For example, the statement

$$probcat = trunc(prob\_1/.00005)$$ **Equation 8.26**

creates a variable *probcat* that corresponds to ranges of values of the predicted probabilities (*prob_1*). Then use the CROSSTABS procedure to calculate Somers' d for the table defined by *probcat* and the variable that designates whether the event of interest occurred. Be sure to suppress the printing of the table, since it will be very large.

Figure 8.21 shows the values of Somers' d for the crosstabulation of predicted probability by actual group membership for this example. (See the Crosstabs chapter in the *SPSS Base Applications Guide* for a discussion of Somers' d.)

Figure 8.21   Somers' d for predicted probability versus group membership

Directional Measures

			Value	Asymp. Std. Error [1]	Approx. T [2]	Approx. Sig.
Ordinal by Ordinal	Somers' d	Symmetric	.447	.070	5.964	.000
		PROBCAT Dependent	.691	.105	5.964	.000
		NODES Dependent	.331	.055	5.964	.000

1. Not assuming the null hypothesis.
2. Using the asymptotic standard error assuming the null hypothesis.

You are interested in the Somers' d that considers *probcat* to be the dependent variable, since you want to eliminate all pairs in which both members experience or don't experience the event. The value of Somers' d with *probcat* dependent is 0.691. To calculate the c statistic, divide Somers' d by 2 and add 0.5. For this example, the c statistic is 0.85. This means that in about 85% of all possible pairs of cases in which one case has positive nodes and the other does not, the logistic regression model assigns a higher probability of having positive nodes to the case with positive nodes.

Model Calibration

Model calibration tells you how closely the observed and predicted probabilities match. A commonly used test for the goodness of fit of the observed and predicted number of events is the Hosmer and Lemeshow test. (Hosmer and Lemeshow, 1989). You divide the cases into 10 approximately equal groups based on the estimated probability of the event occurring (deciles of risk) and see how the observed and expected numbers of events and non-events compare. The chi-square test is used to assess the difference between the observed and expected numbers of events. To use this technique sensibly you must have a fairly large sample size so that the expected number of events in most groups exceeds 5 and none of the groups have expected values less than 1. Since the prostate data set is too small for the test to be useful, we'll consider survival data from 1085 patients hospitalized for septicemia, a life-threatening infection of the blood stream.[1]

Figure 8.22   Hosmer-Lemeshow goodness-of-fit test

```
---------- Hosmer and Lemeshow Goodness-of-Fit Test-----------

        DEAD    = 0            DEAD     = 1

Group   Observed   Expected   Observed   Expected     Total

  1     103.000    103.471     2.000      1.529     105.000
  2     103.000    105.532     6.000      3.468     109.000
  3     103.000    103.893     6.000      5.107     109.000
  4     109.000    109.991    10.000      9.009     119.000
  5      90.000     87.575     8.000     10.425      98.000
  6      94.000     96.363    17.000     14.637     111.000
  7      97.000     90.847    12.000     18.153     109.000
  8      84.000     85.830    26.000     24.170     110.000
  9      79.000     73.717    30.000     35.283     109.000
 10      36.000     40.781    70.000     65.219     106.000

                Chi-Square    df Significance

Goodness-of-fit test    8.1706     8        .4170
-------------------------------------------------------------
```

Figure 8.22 shows the Hosmer and Lemeshow goodness-of-fit test for a logistic regression model that predicts death from septicemia. The cases are divided into 10 approximately equal groups, based on the values for the predicted probability of death. The number of cases in each group is shown in the *Total* column. The groups are not exactly equal since cases with the same combination of values for the independent variables are kept in the same group. For each group, the observed and predicted number of deaths and the observed and predicted number of survivors are shown. For example, in the first

---

1. Thanks to Michael Pine of Michael Pine and Associates for allowing use of these data.

group of 105 cases, 2 died and 103 survived. Summing the predicted probabilities of death for these 105 cases, the predicted number of deaths is 1.53 and the predicted number of survivors is 103.47.

To calculate the Hosmer and Lemeshow goodness-of-fit chi-square, you compute the difference between the observed and predicted number of cases in each of the cells. You then calculate $(O - E)^2 / E$ for each of the cells in the table. The chi-square value is the sum of this quantity over all of the cells. For this example, the chi-square value is 8.17 with 8 degrees of freedom. (The degrees of freedom are calculated as the number of groups minus 2). The observed significance level for the chi-square value is 0.42, so you do not reject the null hypothesis that there is no difference between the observed and predicted values. The model appears to fit the data reasonably well.

The value for the Hosmer and Lemeshow statistic depends on how the cases are grouped. If there is a small number of groups, the test will usually indicate that the model fits, even if it does not. If you have a very large number of cases, the value of the Hosmer and Lemeshow statistic can be large, even if the model fits well, since the value of a chi-square statistic is proportional to sample size. In summary, the Hosmer and Lemeshow statistic provides useful information about the calibration of the model, but it must be interpreted with care.

9 Multinomial Logistic Regression Examples

When you have a dependent variable that is **binary**—it can have only two values—you can use binary logistic regression to model the relationship between the dependent variable and a set of independent variables. For example, you can model the probability that someone will buy your product based on characteristics such as age, education, gender, and income. See Chapter 8 for further discussion of two-group logistic regression.

If you have a categorical dependent variable with more than two possible values, you can use an extension of the binary logistic regression model, called **multinomial** or **polytomous logistic regression**, to examine the relationship between the dependent variable and a set of predictor variables. The models are called multinomial since for each combination of values (or covariate pattern) of the independent variables, the counts of the dependent variable are assumed to have a multinomial distribution. The counts at the different combinations are also assumed to be independent with a fixed total. You can use multinomial logistic regression to study the relationship between marital status and socioeconomic and psychological measures. If your dependent variable is ordinal (such as severe, moderate, and minimal), special types of logistic regression models may be useful (see Agresti, 1990).

SPSS has two procedures that can be used to build logistic regression models: the Binary Logistic Regression procedure and the Multinomial Logistic Regression procedure. Both procedures can be used to build binary regression models. See Chapter 1 for a discussion of differences between the two procedures. The SPSS Multinomial Logistic Regression procedure described in this chapter can also be used to analyze data from one-on-one matched case-control studies. These are studies that construct matched pairs of cases—one has experienced the event of interest, the other has not. Case-control studies are often used in medicine to identify predictors of the event. Matched case-control studies are discussed in more detail on p. 76.

The Logit Model

When you have two groups, one that has experienced the event of interest and the other that has not, you can write the logistic regression model as

$$\log\left(\frac{P(event)}{1 - P(event)}\right) = B_0 + B_1X_1 + B_2X_2 + \dots + B_pX_p$$

where B_0 is the intercept, B_1 to B_p are the logistic regression coefficients, and X_1 to X_p are the independent variables. The quantity on the left side of the equals sign is called a **logit**. It is the natural log of the odds that the event will occur. When the dependent variable has only two values, there is only one nonredundant logit that can be formed. That is because modeling the logit $\log((1 - P(event))/P(event))$ would result in the same logistic regression coefficients for the independent variables, but the signs would be reversed.

If your dependent variable has J possible values, the number of nonredundant logits you can form is $J - 1$. The simplest type of logit for this situation is called the **baseline category logit**. It compares each category to a baseline category. See Agresti (1990) for discussion of logit types when the dependent variable is ordinal. If the baseline category is J, for the ith category, the model is

$$\log\left(\frac{P(category_i)}{P(category_J)}\right) = B_{i0} + B_{i1}X_1 + B_{i2}X_2 + \dots + B_{ip}X_p$$

You will have a set of coefficients for each logit. That's why each coefficient has two subscripts: the first identifies the logit and the second identifies the variable. For the baseline category, the coefficients are all 0. For example, if the dependent variable has three values, you will generate two sets of nonzero coefficients, one for the comparison of each of the first two groups to the last group.

Baseline Logit Example

As an example of multinomial logistic regression, we'll look at the 1992 presidential race. The 1996 General Social Survey asked people whom they voted for in 1992. This data set can be found in *voter.sav*.

From the menus choose:

Analyze
 Descriptive Statistics
  Crosstabs...

▶ Row(s): sex

▶ Column(s): pres92

Cells

 Percentages
  ☑ Row

Figure 9.1   Crosstabulation of the responses by gender

RESPONDENTS SEX * VOTE FOR CLINTON, BUSH, PEROT Crosstabulation

			VOTE FOR CLINTON, BUSH, PEROT			
			Bush	Perot	Clinton	Total
RESPONDENTS SEX	male	Count	315	152	337	804
		% within RESPONDENTS SEX	39.2%	18.9%	41.9%	100.0%
	female	Count	346	126	571	1043
		% within RESPONDENTS SEX	33.2%	12.1%	54.7%	100.0%
Total		Count	661	278	908	1847
		% within RESPONDENTS SEX	35.8%	15.1%	49.2%	100.0%

Figure 9.1 is a crosstabulation of the responses by gender. From the row percentages, you see that 42% of the men and 55% of the women voted for Clinton. Let's consider a simple multinomial logistic regression model to study the relationship between presidential choice and gender.

Since the dependent variable has three categories, two nonredundant logits can be formed using Clinton as the base or reference category and gender as the single independent variable:

$$g_1 = \log\left(\frac{P(\text{Bush})}{P(\text{Clinton})}\right) = B_{10} + B_{11}(male)$$

$$g_2 = \log\left(\frac{P(\text{Perot})}{P(\text{Clinton})}\right) = B_{20} + B_{21}(male)$$

The gender variable has two values, so we arbitrarily select *female* as the reference category and set the coefficients for females to 0. The SPSS Multinomial Logistic Regression procedure treats the last category of a categorical or factor variable as the reference category. In the General Social Survey, males are coded with 1 and females are coded with 2, so *female* is the reference category.

Parameter Estimates

From the menus choose:

Analyze
  Regression
    Multinomial Logistic...

▶ Dependent: pres92

▶ Factor(s): sex

Statistics
  ☐ Summary statistics (deselect)
  ☐ Likelihood ratio test (deselect)
  ☑ Parameter estimates (default)
  Confidence interval: 95% (default)

Figure 9.2   Parameter estimates for model with intercept and gender

Parameter Estimates

VOTE FOR CLINTON, BUSH, PEROT		B	Std. Error	Wald	df	Sig.	Exp(B)	95% Confidence Interval for Exp(B) Lower Bound	Upper Bound
Bush	Intercept	-.501	.068	54.067	1	.000			
	[SEX=1]	.433	.104	17.422	1	.000	1.543	1.258	1.891
	[SEX=2]	0ᵃ	0	.	0	.	.	.	.
Perot	Intercept	-1.511	.098	235.703	1	.000			
	[SEX=1]	.715	.139	26.572	1	.000	2.044	1.558	2.682
	[SEX=2]	0ᵃ	0	.	0	.	.	.	.

a. This parameter is set to 0 because it is redundant.

The two sets of logistic regression coefficients are shown in Figure 9.2. Using these co-efficients, the logit equations can be written as

$$g_1 = \log\left(\frac{P(\text{Bush})}{P(\text{Clinton})}\right) = -0.50 + 0.433(male)$$

$$g_2 = \log\left(\frac{P(\text{Perot})}{P(\text{Clinton})}\right) = -1.51 + 0.715(male)$$

where *male* is 1 for men, 0 for women.

The intercept terms are simply the logits for females. For example, the first intercept is the log of the ratio of the probability of a female choosing Bush to the probability of a female choosing Clinton, or $\log(346/571)$. The second intercept is the log of the ratio of the probability of a female choosing Perot to the probability of a female choosing Clinton. The coefficients for male tell you about the relationship between the logits and gender. Since both coefficients are positive and significantly different from 0, you know that males are more likely than females to select both Bush and Perot as compared to Clinton. In fact, as you can see from the column labeled *Exp(B)*, a male is 1.54 times more likely than a female to choose Bush than Clinton, and 2.04 times more likely than a female to choose Perot than Clinton. See "Interpreting the Regression Coefficients" on p. 40 in Chapter 8 for a more detailed discussion.

Obtaining the Third Pairwise Comparison

The coefficients in Figure 9.2 describe the relationship between gender and the two logits, with Clinton as the reference category. However, there is an additional pairwise comparison that you can make—Bush to Perot. Since this is a redundant logit, you can obtain the coefficients for this comparison as the difference of the two sets of coefficients you have already estimated. That's because

$$\log\left(\frac{P(\text{Bush})}{P(\text{Perot})}\right) = \log\left(\frac{P(\text{Bush})}{P(\text{Clinton})}\right) - \log\left(\frac{P(\text{Perot})}{P(\text{Clinton})}\right)$$

Remember that $\log(a/b) = \log(a) - \log(b)$. However, if you are interested in this logit, it may be simpler to just recode your data so that Perot is the last category, the reference category. The procedure will then automatically calculate the coefficients and standard errors of interest.

Adding Education to the Model

You have seen that the gender of the voter appears to be related to the candidate selected. Let's see whether years of education is also a significant predictor when it is added to a model that already contains gender.

Recall the Multinomial Logistic Regression dialog box and select:

▶ Factor(s): sex, educ

Figure 9.3   Parameter estimates for gender and years of education

Parameter Estimates

VOTE FOR CLINTON, BUSH, PEROT		B	Std. Error	Wald	df	Sig.	Exp(B)	95% Confidence Interval for Exp(B) Lower Bound	Upper Bound
Bush	Intercept	-.702	.259	7.318	1	.007			
	EDUC	1.466E-02	.018	.656	1	.418	1.015	.979	1.051
	[SEX=1]	.428	.104	16.970	1	.000	1.535	1.252	1.881
	[SEX=2]	0[a]	0	.	0	.	.	.	.
Perot	Intercept	-1.894	.353	28.859	1	.000			
	EDUC	2.716E-02	.024	1.248	1	.264	1.028	.980	1.078
	[SEX=1]	.715	.139	26.396	1	.000	2.043	1.556	2.684
	[SEX=2]	0[a]	0	.	0	.	.	.	.

a. This parameter is set to 0 because it is redundant.

Figure 9.3 contains the parameter estimates for the model with gender and years of education. From this table, you see that including education has not changed the coefficients for gender. You also see that for both logits the coefficient for years of education is not significantly different from 0.

Does that mean that education is not an important predictor of voting choice? Not necessarily. It is certainly possible that education is related to candidate choice but not in a linear fashion. To test this, instead of entering the actual years of education into the model, let's consider highest degree achieved (0 = less than high school, 1= high school, 2 = junior college, 3 = bachelor's, and 4 = graduate degree).

Recall the Multinomial Logistic Regression dialog box and select:

▶ Factor(s): sex, degree

Figure 9.4   Parameter estimates for model with intercept, gender, and highest degree received

Parameter Estimates

VOTE FOR CLINTON BUSH, PEROT		B	Std. Error	Wald	df	Sig.	Exp(B)	95% Confidence Interval for Exp(B) Lower Bound	Upper Bound
Bush	Intercept	-.805	.168	22.879	1	.000			
	[SEX=1]	.458	.105	19.148	1	.000	1.581	1.288	1.941
	[SEX=2]	0ª	0	.	0	.	.	.	.
	[DEGREE=0]	-.198	.228	.760	1	.383	.820	.525	1.281
	[DEGREE=1]	.387	.175	4.913	1	.027	1.473	1.046	2.074
	[DEGREE=2]	.431	.253	2.914	1	.088	1.539	.938	2.525
	[DEGREE=3]	.424	.195	4.745	1	.029	1.529	1.043	2.239
	[DEGREE=4]	0ª	0	.	0	.	.	.	.
Perot	Intercept	-2.188	.264	68.527	1	.000			
	[SEX=1]	.760	.140	29.319	1	.000	2.139	1.624	2.816
	[SEX=2]	0ª	0	.	0	.	.	.	.
	[DEGREE=0]	-.502	.393	1.627	1	.202	.605	.280	1.309
	[DEGREE=1]	.833	.267	9.709	1	.002	2.299	1.362	3.882
	[DEGREE=2]	1.052	.346	9.263	1	.002	2.864	1.454	5.640
	[DEGREE=3]	.804	.291	7.608	1	.006	2.233	1.262	3.953
	[DEGREE=4]	0ª	0	.	0	.	.	.	.

a. This parameter is set to 0 because it is redundant.

From Figure 9.4, you see that the *degree* parameter estimates have an interesting pattern. The first parameter estimate represents people with less than a high school education compared to people with a graduate degree. For both of the logits, you cannot reject the null hypothesis that the coefficients are 0. That is, you don't have enough evidence to conclude that people with less than a high school education and those with graduate degrees voted differently. The next three coefficients represent people who graduated from high school but don't have graduate degrees. Within a logit, the three parameter estimates are fairly similar and all but one of them are significantly different from 0. It appears that these three groups behave similarly to each other but differently from those with a graduate degree. The relationship between highest degree earned and voting preference is nonlinear, with the highest and lowest education levels differing from those in the middle. This is not really a surprising finding. It has been noticed before that Democratic candidates are favored by both those with little formal education and those who have advanced degrees. It may make sense to replace the degree variable with a new binary variable that is coded 1 for less than high school or graduate degree and coded 0 otherwise.

Likelihood-Ratio Test

Recall the Multinomial Logistic Regression dialog box and select:

Statistics
    ☑ Likelihood ratio test
    ☐ Parameter estimates (deselect)

Figure 9.5   Likelihood-ratio tests for model with intercept, gender, and degree

Likelihood Ratio Tests

Effect	-2 Log Likelihood of Reduced Model	Chi-Square	df	Sig.
Intercept	103.601	.000	0	.
SEX	140.753	37.153	2	.000
DEGREE	144.590	40.990	8	.000

The chi-square statistic is the difference in -2 log-likelihoods between the final model and a reduced model. The reduced model is formed by omitting an effect from the final model. The null hypothesis is that all parameters of that effect are 0.

Figure 9.5 contains likelihood-ratio tests for the individual effects in the final model that includes gender and degree. The test for each effect is based on the change in the value of -2 log-likelihood if the effect is removed from the final model. If all coefficients for an effect are 0, this change has a chi-square distribution with degrees of freedom equal to the degrees of freedom for the effect being removed. From Figure 9.5, you can conclude that both gender and degree are significantly related to voting choice. The change in -2 log-likelihood is significant if sex is removed from the model containing the intercept, sex, and degree. There is also a significant change if degree is removed from the model containing the intercept, sex, and degree. The likelihood-ratio tests in Figure 9.5 provide better tests for an effect than those based on the Wald statistics shown in previous tables. That's because tests based on the Wald statistic sometimes fail to correctly reject the null hypothesis when coefficients are large. (See Hauck and Donner, 1977.) Notice also that the likelihood-ratio tests provide overall tests for the effects, while the Wald tests in Figure 9.4 are for each category within a logit. You can obtain tests for linear combinations of parameters using the TEST subcommand in syntax.

Recall the Multinomial Logistic Regression dialog box and select:

Statistics
   ☐ Likelihood ratio test (deselect)

Figure 9.6   Model fitting information

Model Fitting Information

Model	-2 Log Likelihood	Chi-Square	df	Sig.
Intercept Only	178.457			
Final	103.601	74.856	10	.000

From Figure 9.6, you can see the value of the -2 log-likelihood both for the model with only the intercept terms and for the final model. The difference between these values is shown in the column labeled *Chi-Square*. If the observed significance level is small, you can reject the null hypothesis that all coefficients for gender and degree are 0. You can conclude that the final model is significantly better than the intercept-only model. The log-likelihood can be expressed as the sum of a multinomial constant that doesn't depend on the parameters, and the kernel, a quantity that does depend on the parameters. The -2 log-likelihood values in Figure 9.6 include both the constant and the kernel. Many books and programs, including SPSS logistic regression, report only the kernel values. Since most tests are based on differences of log-likelihoods, the constants do not matter. If the number of cases is equal to the number of covariate patterns, the constant is 0.

So far, we have considered the effect of gender and highest degree earned on voting behavior. Both of these variables are significantly related to candidate preference. We've looked at the effects of the variables individually, but we have not considered a possible interaction between gender and highest degree. There is an interaction effect between gender and degree earned if the effect of degree is not the same for men and women. For example, it's possible that highly educated women favored Clinton even more than you would predict based only on the coefficients for gender and education.

Recall the Multinomial Logistic Regression dialog box and select:

Model
   ⊙ Full Factorial

Statistics
   ☑ Likelihood ratio test

Figure 9.7   Likelihood ratio tests for effects in the mode

Likelihood Ratio Tests

Effect	-2 Log Likelihood of Reduced Model	Chi-Square	df	Sig.
Intercept	97.227	.000	0	.
SEX	97.227	.000	0	.
DEGREE	97.227	.000	0	.
SEX * DEGREE	103.601	6.374	8	.605

The chi-square statistic is the difference in -2 log-likelihoods between the final model and a reduced model. The reduced model is formed by omitting an effect from the final model. The null hypothesis is that all parameters of that effect are 0.

From Figure 9.7, you see that when the sex-by-degree interaction is removed from the model, the change in –2 log-likelihood is not large enough to reject the null hypothesis that all of the coefficients associated with the interaction effect are 0. The intercept and main effects of sex and degree are included in the interaction and removing them doesn't change the fit of the model. The likelihood-ratio test is not calculated for these effects.

Calculating Predicted Probabilities and Expected Frequencies

From the logistic regression model coefficients, you can estimate the probability that a person will vote for each of the three candidates. As an example, let's calculate the probability that a man with a bachelor's degree votes for each of the candidates. First, you must estimate the values of each of the three logits, using the values for the intercept and the coefficients for male and bachelor's degree:

$$g_1 = -0.8046 + 0.4582 + 0.4244 = 0.0780$$

$$g_2 = -2.1883 + 0.7601 + 0.8035 = -0.6247$$

$$g_3 = 0$$

Remember that for the reference group (the last group), all coefficients are 0. Then, for each group calculate

$$P(group_i) = \frac{\exp(g_i)}{\sum_{k=1}^{J} \exp(g_k)}$$

The estimated probabilities for a male with a bachelor's degree are

$$P(\text{Bush}) = \frac{1.081}{(1 + 1.081 + 0.535)} = 0.413$$

$$P(\text{Perot}) = \frac{0.535}{(1 + 1.081 + 0.535)} = 0.205$$

$$P(\text{Clinton}) = \frac{1}{(1 + 1.081 + 0.535)} = 0.382$$

There are 160 men with bachelor's degree in our data set. Based on the estimated probabilities, you would predict that 66.1 voted for Bush, 32.8 voted for Perot, and 61.1 voted for Clinton.

Recall the Multinomial Logistic Regression dialog box and select:

Model
  ⊙ Main Effects

Statistics
  ☐ Likelihood ratio test (deselect)
  ☑ Cell Probabilities

Figure 9.8   Observed and predicted frequencies and residuals for a model with gender and degree

Observed and Predicted Frequencies

HIGHEST DEGREE	GENDER	VOTE FOR	Frequency			Percentage	
			Observed	Predicted	Pearson Residual	Observed	Predicted
bachelor	male	Bush	71	66.108	.785	44.4%	41.3%
		Perot	27	32.743	-1.125	16.9%	20.5%
		Clinton	62	61.149	.138	38.8%	38.2%

The percentages are based on total observed frequencies in each subpopulation.

Only the covariate pattern of males with bachelor degrees is shown in Figure 9.8, the table of observed and predicted frequencies (calculated more precisely). From Figure 9.8, you see that 71 men actually voted for Bush, 27 for Perot, and 62 for Clinton. For each cell, the Pearson residual is also calculated. The Pearson residual is the difference between the observed and predicted cell counts divided by an estimate of the standard deviation. The Pearson residuals are used to assess how well a model fits the observed data. Cells with Pearson residuals greater than 2 in absolute value should be examined to see if there is an identifiable reason why the model does not fit well. None of the residuals in Figure 9.8 are particularly large.

Classification Table

If you classify each case into the group for which it has the highest predicted probability, you can compare the observed and predicted groups.

Recall the Multinomial Logistic Regression dialog box and select:

Statistics
 ☐ Cell Probabilities (deselect)
 ☑ Classification Table

Figure 9.9   Classification table

Classification

Observed	Predicted			
	Bush	Perot	Clinton	Percent Correct
Bush	251	0	410	38.0%
Perot	133	0	145	.0%
Clinton	237	0	671	73.9%
Overall Percentage	33.6%	.0%	66.4%	49.9%

From Figure 9.9, you see that of the 661 people who actually voted for Bush, 251 are correctly assigned to Bush by the model. Only 38% of Bush supporters are correctly classified. None of the Perot voters are correctly classified. Almost three-quarters of the Clinton voters are correctly identified. Overall, about half of the voters are correctly assigned. Does this mean the model doesn't fit? Not necessarily. It is possible for the model to be correct but classification to be poor. When you have groups of unequal sizes, as in this example, cases will be more likely to be classified to the larger groups, regardless of how well the model fits. Although a classification table provides interesting information, by itself it tells you little about how well a model fits the data. (See Hosmer and Lemeshow, 1989, for further discussion.)

Goodness-of-Fit Tests

Whenever you build a model, you are interested in knowing how well it fits the observed data. The Pearson chi-square statistic is often used to assess the discrepancy between observed and expected counts in a multidimensional crosstabulation. It is computed in the usual manner as

$$\chi^2_{Pearson} = \sum_{all\ cells} \frac{(observed\ count - expected\ count)^2}{expected\ count}$$

Large values for the Pearson χ^2 indicate that the model does not fit well. If the observed significance level is small, you can reject the null hypothesis that your model fits the observed data. Another measure of goodness of fit is the deviance chi-square. It is the change in –2 log-likelihood when the model is compared to a *saturated* model—that is, when it is compared to a model that has all main effects and interactions. If the model fits well, the difference between the log-likelihoods should be small, and the observed significance level should be large. For large sample sizes, both goodness-of-fit statistics should be similar.

The degrees of freedom for both statistics depend on the number of distinct observed combinations of the independent variables (often called the number of covariate patterns), the number of independent logits, and the number of parameters estimated. In this example, the two independent variables form 10 cells, all of them with observed counts greater than 0; the number of independent logits is 2; and the number of estimated parameters is 12. The degrees of freedom are the product of the number of observed covariate patterns and the number of independent logits, minus the number of estimated parameters. The degrees of freedom are $(10 \times 2) - 12 = 8$.

Recall the Multinomial Logistic Regression dialog box and select:

Statistics
    ☐ Classification Table (deselect)
    ☑ Goodness of fit chi-square statistics

Figure 9.10   Goodness-of-fit statistics for a model with gender and degree

Goodness-of-Fit

	Chi-Square	df	Sig.
Pearson	6.327	8	.611
Deviance	6.374	8	.605

From Figure 9.10, you see that you cannot reject the null hypothesis that the model fits. Notice that the deviance chi-square in Figure 9.10 is the same as the likelihood-ratio chi-square for the sex-by-degree interaction in Figure 9.7. That's not a coincidence. The saturated model for Figure 9.10 is the model with sex, degree, and the sex-by-degree interaction. In both Figure 9.10 and Figure 9.7, you are looking at the change in –2 log-likelihood when the interaction is removed from the saturated model.

The goodness-of-fit statistics should be used only when there are multiple cases observed for each of the covariate patterns. If most cases have unique covariate patterns, as is often the situation when covariates are not categorical, the goodness-of-fit tests will not have a chi-square distribution, since the expected values for the cells will be small. (See Hosmer and Lemeshow, 1989.)

Another consideration when evaluating the goodness of fit of a model is determining whether to base the goodness-of-fit tests only on covariate patterns defined by variables in the model or to include additional variables that define the table. For example, if voters were cross-classified on the basis of gender, age group, and degree but if the final model included only gender and degree, the values of the goodness-of-fit tests would differ, depending on whether the covariate patterns were combinations of only degree and gender or whether the covariate patterns were combinations of degree, gender, and age group. That's because the saturated models are different in the two situations. The SPSS Multinomial Logistic Regression procedure allows you to specify the variables to be used for the saturated model by specifying them on the subpopulation subcommand. This feature also allows you to calculate the change in –2 log-likelihood when a set of variables is removed from a model. (See Simonoff, 1998, for further discussion.)

Examining the Residuals

As in other statistical procedures, the examination of residuals and other diagnostic statistics plays an important role in the evaluation of the suitability of a particular model. In this release of SPSS, the Multinomial Logistic Regression procedure does not save any diagnostics or provide any diagnostic plots. For certain models, you can use the Logit or Logistic Regression procedure to calculate and examine diagnostic measures.

Pseudo R^2 Measures

In linear models, the R^2 statistic represents the proportion of variability in the dependent variable that can be explained by the independent variables. It is easily calculated and interpreted. For logistic regression models, an easily interpretable measure of the strength of the relationship between the dependent variable and the independent variables is not available, although a variety of measures have been proposed.

Recall the Multinomial Logistic Regression dialog box and select:

Statistics
   ☑ Summary statistics
   ☐ Goodness of fit chi-square statistics (deselect)

Figure 9.11   Pseudo R-square statistics

Pseudo R-Square

Cox and Snell	.040
Nagelkerke	.046
McFadden	.020

SPSS calculates three such pseudo R^2 statistics, as shown in Figure 9.11. The first two are discussed in Chapter 8. McFadden's R^2 is calculated as

$$R^2_{McFadden} = \frac{l(0) - l(B)}{l(0)}$$

where $l(B)$ is the kernel of the log-likelihood of the model, and $l(0)$ is the kernel of the log-likelihood of the intercept-only model. McFadden's R^2 is the proportion of the kernel of the log-likelihood explained by the logistic regression model.

Correcting for Overdispersion

Most statistical procedures for categorical data assume what is called multinomial sampling. However, the parameter estimates obtained from most procedures are the same for sampling under other models, such as the Poisson. Occasionally, data show more variability than you would expect based on the sampling scheme. This is called **overdispersion**. Different causes such as correlated observations or mixtures of different distributions can result in overdispersion. It is possible to estimate constants from the data that you can use to correct the variance-covariance matrix of parameter estimates. (See McCullagh and Nelder, 1989.) The Multinomial Logistic Regression procedure can estimate correction factors for overdispersion. The Wald tests are then based on the corrected values.

Matched Case-Control Studies

Logistic regression models can be used to analyze data from several different experimental designs. For example, you can take a single random sample of people and then determine who experienced the event of interest (cases) and who did not (controls), or you can take two independent samples, one of cases and one of controls. Sampling cases and controls separately is particularly useful for rare events because you can be sure that you will have enough events to analyze. For both of these situations, the coefficients for the independent variables from the usual logistic regression analysis procedures will be correct. However, for the two-sample situation, you will not be able to estimate the probability of the event in the population for various combinations of risk factors unless you know the sampling fractions for the cases and for the controls and adjust the intercept parameter accordingly. (See Hosmer and Lemeshow, 1989.)

Another type of experimental design that can be analyzed with logistic regression is the matched case-control study. In a matched case-control study, each case is paired with one or more controls that have the same values for preselected risk factors (matched factors), such as age or gender. For each case and control, information is also gathered about other possible risk factors (unmatched variables). The advantage of such a design is that differences between cases and controls with respect to an event can then be attributed to the unmatched risk factors. The SPSS Multinomial Logistic Regression procedure can be used to analyze data from matched case-control studies in which each case is paired with a single control. These are sometimes called **1–1 matched case-control studies**.

The Model

Consider a 1–1 matched design in which there are K matched pairs of cases and controls. The risk of an individual experiencing the event has two components: the risk associated with the matched variables and the risk associated with the unmatched variables. For a particular individual, the logit for experiencing the event can be written as

$$\log(\text{odds of event}) = \alpha_k + \sum_{i=1}^{p} B_i X_i$$

where α_k is the risk for the kth pair based on the values of the matched variables, X_1 to X_p are the values of the unmatched independent variables, and B_i is the logistic regression coefficient for the ith unmatched independent variable.

The log of the ratio of the odds that a case will experience the event to the odds that the corresponding control will experience the event can be written as

$$\log\left(\frac{\text{odds of event for case}}{\text{odds of event for control}}\right) = \sum_{i=1}^{p} B_i D_i$$

where B_i is the coefficient for the ith nonmatched independent variable, and D_i is the difference in values between the case and its matched control. The logistic regression coefficients are interpreted the same for matched and unmatched logistic regression analyses.

Creating the Difference Variables

The SPSS Multinomial Logistic Regression procedure can be used to analyze data from 1–1 matched designs, but the data file must be structured in a special way to reflect the pairing. For the paired analysis, the number of cases must be equal to the number of matched pairs, and the variables must be the differences in values between the case and the control. As an example, consider data from Appendix 3 of Hosmer and Lemeshow (1989). These data are available at *http://www-unix.oit.umass.edu/~statdata/data/plowbwt.dat*, (copyright © John Wiley & Sons, Inc.). There are 56 pairs of mothers— one from each pair gave birth to a low-birth-weight baby, and the other did not. The women are matched on age. The variables we will consider are *lwt*, which is the last weight prior to pregnancy; *age*; *race* (1 = *white*, 2 = *black*, 3 = *other*); *smoke* (smoking during pregnancy, 0 = *no*, 1 = *yes*); *ptd* (previous preterm delivery, 0 = *no*, 1 = *yes*); and *ui* (uterine irritability, 0 = *no*, 1 = *yes*).

Figure 9.12   Data values and differences for a case control pair

	LOW	LWT	AGE	RACE	SMOKE	PTD	UI	RACE1	RACE2
Case	1	101	14	3	1	1	0	0	1
Control	0	135	14	1	0	0	0	0	0
Difference		−34		X	1	1	0	0	1

Figure 9.12 shows the data values and differences for one of the matched pairs. Although it seems easy to compute differences, categorical variables with more than two values pose some difficulties. Recall that for many statistical analyses categorical variables must be transformed prior to analysis (see "Categorical Variables" on p. 47 in Chapter 8). The SPSS Binary Logistic Regression and Multinomial Logistic Regression procedures automatically perform the transformation for variables identified as categorical. These variables must be identified as *factors* in the Multinomial Logistic Regression procedure or *categorical* in the Binary Logistic Regression procedure. However, to run a matched case-control analysis, you must create the new variables used to represent a categorical variable and find the differences between these new variables.

Figure 9.13   Indicator coding of RACE

	RACE1	RACE2
White	0	0
Black	1	0
Other	0	1

Consider a simple example. *Race* is a categorical variable with three values, so you will need two variables to represent it. If you use indicator coding with 1 (white) as the reference category, you must create two new variables, say *race1* and *race2*. *Race1* will be coded 1 for blacks; 0, otherwise. *Race2* will be coded 1 for others; 0, otherwise. Figure 9.13 shows the representation of the three race categories. For each case, you must compute the values of *race1* and *race2*. Then, for each case-control pair, you must calculate the difference between *race1* and *race2*, as shown in Figure 9.12, and use these new variables in the analysis. The same procedure must be followed for interaction terms. Interaction variables must be created first and then differenced.

To analyze a matched case-control study in SPSS Multinomial Logistic Regression, you will need a data file in which each observation consists of the differences for the unmatched variables between a case and the corresponding control. You may want to also keep the values for the matched variables on the record so that you can use them in interaction terms. The dependent variable must be set to a constant for all observations, and all of the difference variables must be identified as *covariates*. The intercept must also be suppressed. Matched variables cannot be entered into the model as main effects, since their difference values are 0 for all cases. However, matched variables in their undifferenced form can be included in interaction terms.

Examining the Results

Figure 9.14 Parameter estimates

Parameter Estimates

Low birth weight		B	Std. Error	Wald	df	Sig.	Exp(B)	95% Confidence Interval for Exp(B)	
								Lower Bound	Upper Bound
Yes	SMOKE	1.348	.568	5.631	1	.018	3.849	1.264	11.715
	UI	1.032	.664	2.418	1	.120	2.808	.764	10.316
	PTD	1.563	.706	4.897	1	.027	4.774	1.196	19.061
	RACE1	.861	.643	1.793	1	.181	2.365	.671	8.338
	RACE2	.469	.604	.603	1	.438	1.598	.489	5.219
	LWT	-9.29E-03	.009	1.051	1	.305	.991	.973	1.009

The parameter estimates for the case-control data set are shown in Figure 9.14. Although the original names of the variables are used, all of the variables represent differences between the case and control pairs.

Figure 9.15 Likelihood-ratio tests

Likelihood Ratio Tests

Effect	-2 Log Likelihood of Reduced Model	Chi-Square	df	Sig.
SMOKE	64.422	6.599	1	.010
UI	60.488	2.665	1	.103
PTD	64.030	6.207	1	.013
RACE1	59.680	1.857	1	.173
RACE2	58.440	.617	1	.432
LWT	58.970	1.147	1	.284

The chi-square statistic is the difference in -2 log-likelihoods between the final model and a reduced model. The reduced model is formed by omitting an effect from the final model. The null hypothesis is that all parameters of that effect are 0.

The likelihood-ratio tests for each of the effects are shown in Figure 9.15. The coefficients for all of the variables except last weight are positive. Only smoking and prior preterm delivery are significantly associated with the low-birth-weight outcome. Smoking increases the odds of low birth weight by a factor of 3.8; prior preterm delivery increases the odds of low birth weight by a factor of 4.8. These factors are found in the column labeled *Exp(B)* in Figure 9.14.

Figure 9.16   Model fitting summary

Model Fitting Information

Model	-2 Log Likelihood	Chi-Square	df	Sig.
Null	77.632			
Final	57.823	19.809	6	.003

From Figure 9.16, you can see that the independent variables are significantly associated with the outcome. The change in –2 log-likelihood is significant when the model with all of the variables is compared to the model with no independent variables and no intercept. You cannot use the goodness-of-fit tests to evaluate how well the model fits, since you don't have multiple observations at each combination of values of the differenced variables. All pairs have different combinations of values. Hosmer and Lemeshow (1989) present a detailed discussion of fitting models to these data, as well as assessing the fit of the model.

10

Probit Analysis Examples

How much insecticide does it take to kill a pest? How low does a sale price have to be to induce a consumer to buy a product? In both of these situations, we are concerned with evaluating the potency of a stimulus. In the first example, the stimulus is the amount of insecticide; in the second, it is the sale price of an object. The response we are interested in is all-or-none. An insect is either dead or alive; a sale is made or not. Since all insects and shoppers do not respond in the same way—that is, they have different tolerances for insecticides and sale prices—the problem must be formulated in terms of the proportion responding at each level of the stimulus.

Different mathematical models can be used to express the relationship between the proportion responding and the "dose" of one or more stimuli. In this chapter, we will consider two commonly used models: the probit response model and the logit response model. We will assume that we have one or more stimuli of interest and that each stimulus can have several doses. We expose different groups of individuals to the desired combinations of stimuli. For each combination, we record the number of individuals exposed and the number who respond.

Probit and Logit Response Models

In probit and logit models, instead of regressing the actual proportion responding on the values of the stimuli, we transform the proportion responding using either a logit or probit transformation. For a probit transformation, we replace each of the observed proportions with the value of the standard normal curve below which the observed proportion of the area is found.

For example, if half (0.5) of the subjects respond at a particular dose, the corresponding probit value is 0, since half of the area in a standard normal curve falls below a Z score of 0. If the observed proportion is 0.95, the corresponding probit value is 1.64.

If the logit transformation is used, the observed proportion P is replaced by

$$\ln\left(\frac{P}{1-P}\right)$$

Equation 10.1

This quantity is called a **logit**. If the observed proportion is 0.5, the logit-transformed value is 0, the same as the probit-transformed value. Similarly, if the observed proportion is 0.95, the logit-transformed value is 1.47. This differs somewhat from the corresponding probit value of 1.64. (In most situations, analyses based on logits and probits give very similar results.)

The regression model for the transformed response can be written as

$$\text{Transformed} P_i = A + BX_i \qquad\qquad \textbf{Equation 10.2}$$

where P_i is the observed proportion responding at dose X_i. (Usually, the log of the dose is used instead of the actual dose.) If there is more than one stimulus variable, terms are added to the model for each of the stimuli. The SPSS Probit Analysis procedure obtains maximum-likelihood estimates of the regression coefficients.

An Example

Finney (1971) presents data showing the effect of a series of doses of rotenone (an insecticide) when sprayed on *Macrosiphoniella sanborni*. Table 10.1 contains the concentration, the number of insects tested at each dose, the proportion dying, and the probit transformation of each of the observed proportions.

Table 10.1   Effects of rotenone

Dose	Number observed	Number dead	Proportion dead	Probit
10.2	50	44	0.88	1.18
7.7	49	42	0.86	1.08
5.1	46	24	0.52	0.05
3.8	48	16	0.33	-0.44
2.6	50	6	0.12	-1.18

Figure 10.1 is a plot of the observed probits against the logs of the concentrations. (On the menus, you specify *died* as the response frequency variable, *total* as the observation frequency variable, and *dose* as the covariate. You also ask for a log transformation of *dose*.) You can see that the relationship between the two variables is linear. If the relationship did not appear to be linear, the concentrations would have to be transformed in some other way in order to achieve linearity. If a suitable transformation could not be found, fitting a straight line would not be a reasonable strategy for modeling the data.

Figure 10.1   Plot of observed probits against logs of concentrations

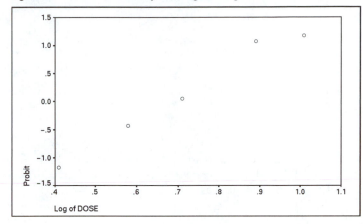

The parameter estimates and standard errors for this example are shown in Figure 10.2.

Figure 10.2   Parameter estimates and standard errors

```
Parameter estimates converged after 10 iterations.
Optimal solution found.

Parameter Estimates (PROBIT model:  (PROBIT(p)) = Intercept + BX):

           Regression Coeff.  Standard Error     Coeff./S.E.

   DOSE            4.16914           .47306         8.81306


                 Intercept   Standard Error   Intercept/S.E.

                 -2.85940          .34717         -8.23640

Pearson  Goodness-of-Fit  Chi Square =      1.621    DF = 3    P =   .655

Since Goodness-of-Fit Chi square is NOT significant, no heterogeneity
factor is used in the calculation of confidence limits.
```

The regression equation is

$$\text{Probit}(P_i) = -2.86 + 4.17(\log_{10}(\text{dose}_i))$$

Equation 10.3

To see how well this model fits, consider Figure 10.3, which contains observed and expected frequencies, residuals, and the predicted probability of a response for each of the log concentrations.

Figure 10.3   Statistics for each concentration

```
Observed and Expected Frequencies

           Number of    Observed    Expected
   DOSE    Subjects    Responses    Responses    Residual    Prob
   1.01      50.0        44.0         45.586      -1.586     .91172
    .89      49.0        42.0         39.330       2.670     .80265
    .71      46.0        24.0         24.845       -.845     .54010
    .58      48.0        16.0         15.816        .184     .32950
    .41      50.0         6.0          6.253       -.253     .12506
```

You can see that the model appears to fit the data reasonably well. A goodness-of-fit test for the model, based on the residuals, is shown in Figure 10.2. The chi-square goodness-of-fit test is calculated as

$$\chi^2 = \sum \frac{(\text{residual}_i)^2}{n_i \hat{P}_i (1 - \hat{P}_i)}$$

Equation 10.4

where n_i is the number of subjects exposed to dose i, and $\hat{P}_i$ is the predicted proportion responding at dose i. The degrees of freedom are equal to the number of doses minus the number of estimated parameters. In this example, we have five doses and two estimated parameters, so there are three degrees of freedom for the chi-square statistic. Since the observed significance level for the chi-square statistic is large—0.655—there is no reason to doubt the model.

When the significance level of the chi-square statistic is small, several explanations are possible. It may be that the relationship between the concentration and the probit is not linear. Or it may be that the relationship is linear but the spread of the observed points around the regression line is unequal. That is, the data are heterogeneous. If this is the case, a correction must be applied to the estimated variances for each concentration group (see "Confidence Intervals for Expected Dosages" below).

Confidence Intervals for Expected Dosages

Often you want to know what the concentration of an agent must be in order to achieve a certain proportion of response. For example, you may want to know what the concentration would have to be in order to kill half of the insects. This is known as the **median lethal dose**. It can be obtained from the previous regression equation by solving for the concentration that corresponds to a probit value of 0. For this example,

$$\log_{10}(\text{median lethal dose}) = 2.86/4.17$$

$$\text{median lethal dose} = 4.85$$

Equation 10.5

Confidence intervals can be constructed for the median lethal dose as well as for the dose required to achieve any response. The SPSS Probit Analysis procedure calculates 95% intervals for the concentrations required to achieve various levels of response. The values for this example are shown in Figure 10.4.

Figure 10.4   Confidence intervals

Confidence Limits for Effective DOSE

Prob	DOSE	95% Confidence Limits Lower	Upper
.01	1.34232	.90152	1.73955
.02	1.56042	1.09195	1.97144
.03	1.71682	1.23282	2.13489
.04	1.84473	1.35041	2.26709
.05	1.95577	1.45411	2.38094
.06	2.05553	1.54847	2.48260
.07	2.14718	1.63607	2.57552
.08	2.23270	1.71858	2.66189
.09	2.31344	1.79709	2.74314
.10	2.39033	1.87239	2.82033
.15	2.73686	2.21737	3.16638
.20	3.04775	2.53300	3.47603
.25	3.34246	2.83556	3.77074
.30	3.63134	3.13342	4.06251
.35	3.92126	3.43173	4.36004
.40	4.21775	3.73415	4.67105
.45	4.52592	4.04368	5.00346
.50	4.85119	4.36322	5.36609
.55	5.19983	4.69624	5.76942
.60	5.57976	5.04753	6.22651
.65	6.00164	5.42413	6.75456
.70	6.48081	5.83681	7.37806
.75	7.04092	6.30250	8.13488
.80	7.72177	6.84956	9.08968
.85	8.59893	7.53102	10.36751
.90	9.84550	8.46614	12.26163
.91	10.17274	8.70644	12.77237
.92	10.54059	8.97434	13.35269
.93	10.96042	9.27744	14.02276
.94	11.44911	9.62693	14.81270
.95	12.03312	10.04028	15.77021
.96	12.75742	10.54699	16.97720
.97	13.70788	11.20286	18.59208
.98	15.08186	12.13489	20.98491
.99	17.53233	13.75688	25.40958

The column labeled *Prob* is the proportion responding. The column labeled *DOSE* is the estimated dosage required to achieve this proportion. The 95% confidence limits for the dose are shown in the next two columns. If the chi-square goodness-of-fit test has a significance level less than 0.15 (the program default), a heterogeneity correction is automatically included in the computation of the intervals (Finney, 1971).

Comparing Several Groups

In the previous example, only one stimulus at several doses was studied. If you want to compare several different stimuli, each measured at several doses, additional statistics may be useful. Consider the inclusion of two additional insecticides in the previously described problem. Besides rotenone at five concentrations, we also have five concentrations of deguelin and four concentrations of a mixture of the two. Figure 10.5 shows a partial listing of these data, as entered in the Data Editor. As in the previous example, variable *dose* contains the insecticide concentration, *total* contains the total number of cases, and *died* contains the number of deaths. Factor variable *agent* is coded 1 (roten-one), 2 (deguelin), or 3 (mixture).

Figure 10.5　Data for rotenone and deguelin

	dose	agent	total	died
1	2.57	1.00	50.00	6.00
2	3.80	1.00	48.00	16.00
3	5.13	1.00	46.00	24.00
4	7.76	1.00	49.00	42.00
5	10.23	1.00	50.00	44.00
6	10.00	2.00	48.00	18.00
7	20.42	2.00	48.00	34.00
8	30.20	2.00	49.00	47.00
9	40.74	2.00	50.00	47.00
10	50.12	2.00	48.00	48.00

Figure 10.6 is a plot of the observed probits against the logs of the concentrations for each of the three groups separately.

Figure 10.6　Plot of observed probits against logs of concentrations

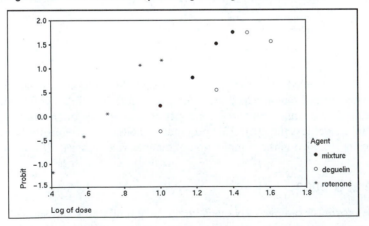

You can see that there appears to be a linear relationship between the two variables for all three groups. One of the questions of interest is whether all three lines are parallel. If so, it would make sense to estimate a common slope for them. Figure 10.7 contains the estimate of the common slope, separate intercept estimates for each of the groups, and a test of parallelism.

Figure 10.7   Intercept estimates and test of parallelism

```
           Regression Coeff.   Standard Error      Coeff./S.E.

DOSE              3.90635              .30691         12.72803


              Intercept    Standard Error   Intercept/S.E.   AGENT

               -2.67343          .23577        -11.33913     rotenone
               -4.36573          .40722        -10.72071     deguelin
               -3.71153          .37491         -9.89977     mixture

Pearson  Goodness-of-Fit  Chi Square =       7.471   DF = 24   P =  .999
         PARALLELISM TEST CHI SQUARE =       1.162   DF = 2    P =  .559

Since Goodness-of-Fit Chi square is NOT significant, no heterogeneity
factor is used in the calculation of confidence limits.
```

The observed significance level for the test of parallelism is large—0.559—so there is no reason to reject the hypothesis that all three lines are parallel. Thus, the equation for rotenone is estimated to be

$$\text{Probit}(P_i) = -2.67 + 3.91(\log_{10}(\text{dose}_i)) \qquad \textbf{Equation 10.6}$$

The equation for deguelin is

$$\text{Probit}(P_i) = -4.37 + 3.91(\log_{10}(\text{dose}_i)) \qquad \textbf{Equation 10.7}$$

and the equation for the mixture is

$$\text{Probit}(P_i) = -3.71 + 3.91(\log_{10}(\text{dose}_i)) \qquad \textbf{Equation 10.8}$$

Comparing Relative Potencies of the Agents

The relative potency of two stimuli is defined as the ratio of two doses that are equally effective. For example, the relative median potency is the ratio of two doses that achieve a response rate of 50%. In the case of parallel regression lines, there is a constant relative potency at all levels of response. For example, consider Figure 10.8, which shows some of the doses needed to achieve a particular response for each of the three agents.

Figure 10.8 Expected doses

```
AGENT      1  rotenone

                         95% Confidence Limits
Prob         DOSE        Lower          Upper

.25        3.24875       2.82553        3.65426
.30        3.54926       3.11581        3.97227
.35        3.85249       3.40758        4.29636
.40        4.16414       3.70545        4.63356
.45        4.48965       4.01370        4.99083
.50        4.83482       4.33680        5.37586
.55        5.20654       4.68002        5.79788
.60        5.61352       5.05003        6.26880
.65        6.06764       5.45592        6.80487
.70        6.58603       5.91086        7.42974
.75        7.19524       6.43524        8.18030


AGENT      2  deguelin

                         95% Confidence Limits
Prob         DOSE        Lower          Upper

.25        8.80913       7.24085       10.32755
.30        9.62399       8.00041       11.20430
.35       10.44620       8.76976       12.09054
.40       11.29127       9.56202       13.00451
.45       12.17389      10.38960       13.96387
.50       13.10986      11.26577       14.98799
.55       14.11778      12.20605       16.10010
.60       15.22135      13.23000       17.33026
.65       16.45271      14.36393       18.71981
.70       17.85833      15.64554       20.32922
.75       19.51024      17.13277       22.25327


AGENT      3  mixture

                         95% Confidence Limits
Prob         DOSE        Lower          Upper

.25        5.99049       4.82754        7.12052
.30        6.54462       5.33737        7.72006
.35        7.10375       5.85480        8.32478
.40        7.67843       6.38880        8.94696
.45        8.27864       6.94795        9.59841
.50        8.91512       7.54150       10.29194
.55        9.60054       8.18034       11.04290
.60       10.35100       8.87822       11.87107
.65       11.18837       9.65364       12.80367
.70       12.14424      10.53309       13.88054
.75       13.26759      11.55720       15.16421
```

For rotenone, the expected dosage to kill half of the insects is 4.83; for deguelin, it is 13.11; and for the mixture, it is 8.91. The relative median potency for rotenone compared to deguelin is $4.83/13.11$, or 0.37; for rotenone compared to the mixture, it is 0.54; and for deguelin compared to the mixture, it is 1.47. These relative median potencies and their confidence intervals are shown in Figure 10.9.

Figure 10.9 Relative potencies and their confidence intervals

```
Estimates of Relative Median Potency

                            95% Confidence Limits
  AGENT        Estimate       Lower        Upper

1 VS.   2        .3688       .23353       .52071
1 VS.   3        .5423       .38085       .71248
2 VS.   3       1.4705      1.20619      1.85007
```

If a confidence interval does not include the value of 1, we have reason to suspect the hypothesis that the two agents are equally potent.

Estimating the Natural Response Rate

In some situations, the response of interest is expected to occur even if the stimulus is not present. For example, if the organism of interest has a very short life span, you would expect to observe deaths even without the agent. In such situations, you must adjust the observed proportions to reflect deaths due to the agent alone.

If the natural response rate is known, it can be entered into the SPSS Probit Analysis procedure. It can also be estimated from the data, provided that data for a dose of 0 are entered together with the other doses. If the natural response rate is estimated from the data, an additional degree of freedom must be subtracted from the chi-square goodness-of-fit degrees of freedom.

More than One Stimulus Variable

If several stimuli are evaluated simultaneously, an additional term is added to the regression model for each stimulus. Regression coefficients and standard errors are displayed for each stimulus. In the case of several stimuli, relative potencies and confidence intervals for the doses needed to achieve a particular response cannot be calculated in the usual fashion, since you need to consider various combinations of the levels of the stimuli.

11 Nonlinear Regression Examples

Many real-world relationships are approximated with linear models, especially in the absence of theoretical models that can serve as guides. We would be unwise to model the relationship between speed of a vehicle and stopping time with a linear model, since the laws of physics dictate otherwise. However, nothing deters us from modeling salary as a linear function of variables such as age, education, and experience. In general, we choose the simplest model that fits an observed relationship. Another reason that explains our affinity to linear models is the accompanying simplicity of statistical estimation and hypothesis testing. Algorithms for estimating parameters of linear models are straightforward; direct solutions are available; iteration is not required. There are, however, situations in which it is necessary to fit nonlinear models. Before considering the steps involved in nonlinear model estimation, let's consider what makes a model nonlinear.

What Is a Nonlinear Model?

There is often confusion about the characteristics of a nonlinear model. Consider the following equation:

$$Y = B_0 + B_1 X_1^2$$

Equation 11.1

Is this a linear or nonlinear model? The equation is certainly not that of a straight line—it is the equation for a parabola. However, the word *linear,* in this context, does not refer to whether the equation is that of a straight line or a curve. It refers to the functional form of the equation. That is, can the dependent variable be expressed as a linear combination of parameter values times values of the independent variables? The parameters must be linear. The independent variables can be transformed in any fashion. They can be raised to various powers, logged, and so on. The transformation cannot involve the parameters in any way, however.

The previous model is a linear model, since it is nonlinear in only the independent variable X. It is linear in the parameters B_0 and B_1. In fact, we can write the model as

$$Y = B_0 + B_1 X'$$

Equation 11.2

where X' is the square of X_1. The parameters in the model can be estimated using the usual linear model techniques.

Transforming Nonlinear Models

Consider the model

$$Y = e^{B_0 + B_1 X_1 + B_2 X_2 + E}$$ **Equation 11.3**

The model, as it stands, is not of the form

$$Y = B_0 + B_1 Z_1 + B_2 Z_2 + \ldots + B_p Z_p + E$$ **Equation 11.4**

where the B's are the parameters and the Z's are functions of the independent variables, so it is a nonlinear model. However, if we take natural logs of both sides of Equation 11.3, we get the model

$$\ln(Y) = B_0 + B_1 X_1 + B_2 X_2 + E$$ **Equation 11.5**

The transformed equation is linear in the parameters, and we can use the usual techniques for estimating them. Models that initially appear to be nonlinear but that can be transformed to a linear form are sometimes called **intrinsically linear models**. It is a good idea to examine what appears to be a nonlinear model to see if it can be transformed to a linear one. Transformation to linearity makes estimation much easier.

Another example of a transformable nonlinear model is

$$Y = e^B X + E$$ **Equation 11.6**

The transformation $B' = e^B$ results in the model

$$Y = B'X + E$$ **Equation 11.7**

We can use the usual methods to estimate B' and then take its natural log to get the values of B.

Error Terms in Transformed Models

In both linear and nonlinear models, we assume that the error term is additive. When we transform a model to linearity, we must make sure that the transformed error term satisfies the requisite assumptions. For example, if our original model is

$$Y = e^{BX} + E$$ **Equation 11.8**

taking natural logs does not result in a model that has an additive error term. To have an additive error term in the transformed model, our original model would have had to be

$$Y = e^{BX + E} = e^{BX} e^E$$

Equation 11.9

Intrinsically Nonlinear Models

A model such as

$$Y = B_0 + e^{B_1 X_1} + e^{B_2 X_2} + e^{B_3 X_3} + E$$

Equation 11.10

is **intrinsically nonlinear**. We can't apply a transformation to linearize it. We must estimate the parameters using nonlinear regression. In nonlinear regression, just as in linear regression, we choose values for the parameters so that the sum of squared residuals is a minimum. There is not, however, a closed solution. We must solve for the values iteratively. There are several algorithms for the estimation of nonlinear models (see Fox, 1984; Draper and Smith, 1981).

Fitting the Logistic Population Growth Model

As an example of fitting a nonlinear equation, we will consider a model for population growth. Population growth is often modeled using a logistic population growth model of the form

$$Y_i = \frac{C}{1 + e^{A + BT_i}} + E_i$$

Equation 11.11

where Y_i is the population size at time T_i. Although the model often fits the observed data reasonably well, the assumptions of independent error and constant variance may be violated because, with time series data, errors are not independent and the size of the error may be dependent on the magnitude of the population. Since the logistic population growth model is not transformable to a linear model, we will have to use nonlinear regression to estimate the parameters.

Figure 11.1 contains a listing of decennial populations (in millions) of the United States from 1790 to 1960, as found in Fox (1984). Figure 11.2 is a plot of the same data. For the nonlinear regression, we will use the variable *decade*, which represents the number of decades since 1790, as the independent variable. This should prevent possible computational difficulties arising from large data values (see "Computational Problems" on p. 100).

Figure 11.1   Decennial population of the United States

```
POP  YEAR DECADE

  3.895 1790     0
  5.267 1800     1
  7.182 1810     2
  9.566 1820     3
 12.834 1830     4
 16.985 1840     5
 23.069 1850     6
 31.278 1860     7
 38.416 1870     8
 49.924 1880     9
 62.692 1890    10
 75.734 1900    11
 91.812 1910    12
109.806 1920    13
122.775 1930    14
131.669 1940    15
150.697 1950    16
178.464 1960    17
```

Figure 11.2   Plot of decennial population of the United States

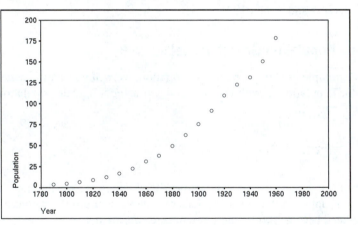

In order to start the nonlinear estimation algorithm, we must have initial values for the parameters. Unfortunately, the results of nonlinear estimation often depend on having good starting values for the parameters. There are several ways for obtaining starting values (see "Estimating Starting Values" on p. 98 through "Use Properties of the Nonlinear Model" on p. 99).

For this example, we can obtain starting values by making some simple assumptions. In the logistic growth model, the parameter C represents the asymptote. We'll arbitrarily choose an asymptote that is not too far from the largest observed value. Let's take an asymptote of 200, since the largest observed value for the population is 178.

Using the value of 200 for C, we can estimate a value for A based on the observed population at time 0:

$$3.895 = \frac{200}{1 + e^A}$$

Equation 11.12

So,

$$A = \ln\left(\frac{200}{3.895} - 1\right) = 3.9$$

Equation 11.13

To estimate a value for B, we can use the population at time 1, and our estimates of C and A. This gives us

$$5.267 = \frac{200}{1 + e^{B + 3.9}}$$

Equation 11.14

from which we derive

$$B = \ln\left(\frac{200}{5.27} - 1\right) - 3.9 = -0.29$$

Equation 11.15

We use these values as initial values in the nonlinear regression routine.

Estimating the Parameters

Figure 11.3 shows the residual sums of squares and parameter estimates at each iteration. At step 1, the parameter estimates are the starting values that we have supplied. At the major iterations, which are identified with integer numbers, the derivatives are evaluated and the direction of the search determined. At the minor iterations, the distance is established. As the note at the end of the table indicates, iteration stops when the relative change in residual sums of squares between iterations is less than or equal to the convergence criterion.

Figure 11.3 Parameter estimates for nonlinear regression

Iteration	Residual SS	A	B	C
1	969.6898219	3.90000000	-.30000000	200.000000
1.1	240.3756627	3.87148504	-.27852485	237.513990
2	240.3756627	3.87148504	-.27852485	237.513990
2.1	186.5020615	3.89003377	-.27910189	243.721558
3	186.5020615	3.89003377	-.27910189	243.721558
3.1	186.4972404	3.88880287	-.27886478	243.975460
4	186.4972404	3.88880287	-.27886478	243.975460
4.1	186.4972278	3.88885123	-.27886164	243.985980
5	186.4972278	3.88885123	-.27886164	243.985980
5.1	186.4972277	3.88884856	-.27886059	243.987296

Run stopped after 10 model evaluations and 5 derivative evaluations.
Iterations have been stopped because the relative reduction between successive residual sums of squares is at most SSCON = 1.000E-08

Summary statistics for the nonlinear regression are shown in Figure 11.4. For a nonlinear model, the tests used for linear models are not appropriate. In this situation, the residual mean square is not an unbiased estimate of the error variance, even if the model is correct. For practical purposes, we can still compare the residual variance with an estimate of the total variance, but the usual F statistic cannot be used for testing hypotheses.

The entry in Figure 11.4 labeled *Uncorrected Total* is the sum of the squared values of the dependent variable. The entry labeled *(Corrected Total)* is the sum of squared deviations around the mean. The *Regression* sum of squares is the sum of the squared predicted values. The entry labeled *R squared* is the coefficient of determination. It may be interpreted as the proportion of the total variation of the dependent variable around its mean that is explained by the fitted model. For nonlinear models, its value can be negative if the selected model fits worse than the mean. (For a discussion of this statistic, see Kvalseth, 1985.) It appears from the R^2 value of 0.9965 that the model fits the observed values well. Figure 11.5 is a plot of the observed and predicted values for the model.

Figure 11.4   Summary statistics for nonlinear regression

```
Nonlinear Regression Summary Statistics       Dependent Variable POP

   Source               DF   Sum of Squares   Mean Square

   Regression            3    123053.53112     41017.84371
   Residual             15       186.49723        12.43315
   Uncorrected Total    18    123240.02834

   (Corrected Total)    17     53293.92477

   R squared = 1 - Residual SS / Corrected SS =     .99650
```

Figure 11.5   Observed and predicted values for nonlinear model

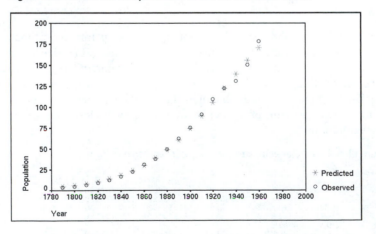

Approximate Confidence Intervals for the Parameters

In the case of nonlinear regression, it is not possible to obtain exact confidence intervals for each of the parameters. Instead, we must rely on **asymptotic** (large sample) approximations. Figure 11.6 shows the estimated parameters, standard errors, and asymptotic 95% confidence intervals. The asymptotic correlation matrix of the parameter estimates is shown in Figure 11.7. If there are very large positive or negative values for the correlation coefficients, it is possible that the model is **overparameterized**. That is, a model with fewer parameters may fit the observed data as well. This does not necessarily mean that the model is inappropriate; it may mean that the amount of data is not sufficient to estimate all of the parameters.

Figure 11.6   Estimated parameters and confidence intervals

Parameter	Estimate	Asymptotic Std. Error	Asymptotic 95 % Confidence Interval Lower	Upper
A	3.888848562	.093704407	3.689122346	4.088574778
B	-.278860588	.015593951	-.312098308	-.245622868
C	243.98729636	17.967399750	205.69069033	282.28390239

Figure 11.7   Asymptotic correlation matrix of parameter estimates

Asymptotic Correlation Matrix of the Parameter Estimates

	A	B	C
A	1.0000	-.7244	-.3762
B	-.7244	1.0000	.9042
C	-.3762	.9042	1.0000

Examining the Residuals

The SPSS Nonlinear Regression procedure allows you to save predicted values and residuals that can be used for exploring the goodness of fit of the model. Figure 11.8 is a plot of residuals against the observed year values. You will note that the errors appear to be correlated and that the variance of the residuals increases with time.

Figure 11.8   Plot of residuals against observed values

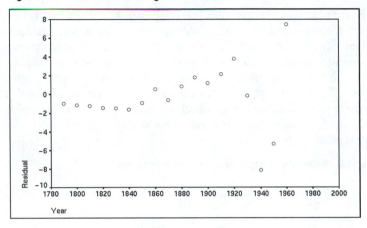

To compute asymptotic standard errors of the predicted values and statistics used for outlier detection and influential case analysis, you can use the SPSS Linear Regression procedure, specifying the residuals from the SPSS Nonlinear Regression procedure as the dependent variable and the derivatives as the independent variables.

Estimating Starting Values

As previously indicated, you must specify initial values for all parameters. Good initial values are important and may provide a better solution in fewer iterations. In addition, computational difficulties can sometimes be avoided by a good choice of initial values. Poor initial values can result in nonconvergence, a local rather than global solution, or a physically impossible solution.

There are a number of ways to determine initial values for nonlinear models. Milliken (1987) and Draper and Smith (1981) describe several approaches, which are summarized in the following sections. Generally, a combination of techniques will be most useful. If you don't have starting values, don't just set them all to 0. Use values in the neighborhood of what you expect to see.

If you ignore the error term, sometimes a linear form of the model can be derived. Linear regression can then be used to obtain initial values. For example, consider the model

$$Y = e^{A + BX} + E$$

Equation 11.16

If we ignore the error term and take the natural log of both sides of the equation, we obtain the model

$$\ln(Y) = A + BX$$

Equation 11.17

We can use linear regression to estimate A and B and specify these values as starting values in nonlinear regression.

Use Properties of the Nonlinear Model

Sometimes we know the values of the dependent variable for certain combinations of parameter values. For example, if in the model

$$Y = e^{A + BX}$$

Equation 11.18

we know that when X is 0, Y is 2, we would select the natural log of 2 as a starting value for A. Examination of an equation at its maximum, minimum, and when all the independent variables approach 0 or infinity may help in selection of initial values.

Solve a System of Equations

By taking as many data points as you have parameters, you can solve a simultaneous system of equations. For example, in the previous model, we could solve the equations

$$\ln(Y_1) = A + BX_1$$
$$\ln(Y_2) = A + BX_2$$

Equation 11.19

Using subtraction,

$$\ln(Y_1) - \ln(Y_2) = BX_1 - BX_2$$

Equation 11.20

we can solve for the values of the parameters

$$B = \frac{\ln(Y_1) - \ln(Y_2)}{X_1 - X_2}$$

Equation 11.21

and

$$A = \ln(Y_1) - BX_1$$

Equation 11.22

Computational Problems

Computationally, nonlinear regression problems can be difficult to solve. Models that require exponentiation or powers of large data values may cause underflows or overflows. (An **overflow** is caused by a number that is too large for the computer to handle, while an **underflow** is caused by a number that is too small for the computer to handle.) Sometimes the program may continue and produce a reasonable solution, especially if only a few data points caused the problem. If this is not the case, you must eliminate the cause of the problem. If your data values are large—for example, years—you can subtract the smallest year from all of the values. That's what was done with the population example. Instead of using the actual years, we used decades since 1790 (to compute the number of decades, we subtracted the smallest year from each year value and divided the result by 10). You must, however, consider the effect of rescaling on the parameter values. Many nonlinear models are not scale invariant. You can also consider rescaling the parameter values.

If the program fails to arrive at a solution—that is, if it doesn't converge—you might consider choosing different starting values. You can also change the criterion used for convergence.

If none of these strategies works, you can use the sequential quadratic programming algorithm to try to solve problems that are causing difficulties in the Nonlinear Regression procedure, which uses a Levenberg-Marquardt algorithm by default. For a particular problem, one algorithm may perform better than the other.

Additional Nonlinear Regression Options

Three additional options are available for nonlinear models when the sequential quadratic programming algorithm is used. You can supply linear and nonlinear constraints for the values of the parameter estimates, and you can specify your own loss function. (By default, the loss function that is minimized is the sum of the squared residuals.) In addition, standard errors for the parameter estimates as well as asymptotic confidence intervals can be obtained with **bootstrapping**, in which repeated random samples are selected from the data and the model is estimated from each one.

12 Weighted Least-Squares Regression Examples

When you estimate the parameters of a linear regression model, all observations usually contribute equally to the computations. This is called **ordinary least-squares (OLS) regression**. When all of the observations have the same variance, this is the best strategy because it results in parameter estimates that have the smallest possible variances. However, if the observations are not measured with equal precision, OLS no longer yields parameter estimates with the smallest variance. A modification known as **weighted least-squares (WLS) analysis** does. In weighted least-squares regression, data points are weighted by the reciprocal of their variances. This means that observations with large variances have less impact on the analysis than observations associated with small variances.

An Example

As an example of the use of weighted least squares, consider the data presented in Table 2.1 of Draper and Smith (1981). Figure 12.1 is a plot of the two variables.

Figure 12.1   Plot of y and x

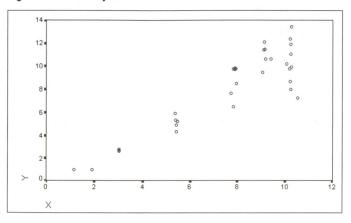

One of the first things you notice is that the variability or spread of the dependent variable increases with increasing values of the independent variable. This indicates that the assumption of equal variances across all data points is probably violated and the ordinary least-squares approach is no longer optimal.

If you were to fit an ordinary least-squares regression to the data points (by running the Linear Regression procedure), you would obtain the output shown in Figure 12.2.

Figure 12.2   Linear Regression output

```
Multiple R              .91659
R Square                .84013
Adjusted R Square       .83529
Standard Error         1.45660


Analysis of Variance
                     DF      Sum of Squares      Mean Square
Regression            1            367.94805      367.94805
Residual             33             70.01571        2.12169

F =       173.42230      Signif F =  .0000

------------------ Variables in the Equation ------------------

Variable              B          SE B        Beta        T   Sig T

X               1.135404     .086218      .916588    13.169  .0000
(Constant)      -.578954     .679186                  -.852  .4001



Residuals Statistics:

               Min       Max      Mean    Std Dev    N

*PRED         .7268   11.3428    7.7569    3.2897    35
*RESID      -4.0928    2.4238     .0000    1.4350    35
*ZPRED      -2.1370    1.0901     .0000    1.0000    35
*ZRESID     -2.8098    1.6640     .0000     .9852    35

Total Cases =          35


From Equation   1:   2 new variables have been created.

   Name        Contents
   ----        --------

   PRE_1        Predicted Value
   RES_1        Residual
```

You can't tell from the coefficients or summary statistics that the requisite regression assumptions are violated. You must examine the residual plots. These are shown in Figure 12.3.

Figure 12.3   Plot of residuals and predicted values

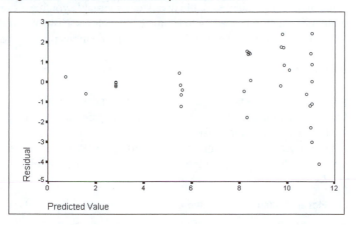

You see that instead of being randomly distributed around the line through 0, the residuals form a funnel, suggesting again that the variances are unequal and that the data must be transformed (see *SPSS Base User's Guide*) or that weighted least squares should be used.

Estimating the Weights from Replicates

In order to estimate the regression model with weighted least squares, you must have an estimate of the variability at each point. Unfortunately, this information is often unavailable and you must estimate the variability from the data. If you have replicates in your data—that is, groups of cases for which the values of the independent variable are the same or similar—you can compute the variances of the dependent variable for all of the distinct combinations of the independent variables. The reciprocal of the variances is then the weight, since you want points associated with large variances to have less impact than points with smaller variances. If you have few observations at each point, the variance estimates based on replicates may not be very reliable.

Estimating Weights from a Variable

If you don't estimate weights from replicates, you can look for a relationship between the variance and the values of other related variables. It is not unusual for the variance of a dependent variable to be related to the magnitude of an independent variable. For example, if you are looking at the relationship between income and education, you may well expect that there will be more variability in income for people with graduate education than for those who did not complete grammar school.

If you think that there is a relationship between the variance of the dependent variable and the value of an independent variable or any other variable you have available, you can use the Weight Estimation procedure to estimate the weights. However, the variance must be proportional to a power of the variable. That is, the relationship must be of the form

variance $\propto$ variable^{power} **Equation 12.1**

You can specify a power range and an increment, and the program will evaluate the log-likelihood function for all powers within the grid and then select the power corresponding to the largest log-likelihood.

In the Draper and Smith example, if you group cases with similar values for the independent variable and compute their standard deviations, you obtain the plot shown in Figure 12.4.

Figure 12.4   Plot of standard deviation and x

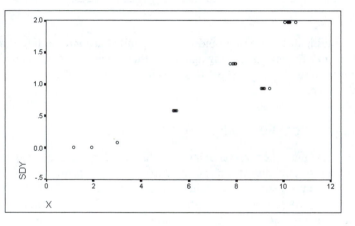

It appears that the standard deviation of y is linearly related to x. That means the variance is related to the square of x.

If you run the Weight Estimation procedure with x as the weight variable and power ranging from 0 to 3 in increments of 0.2, you will obtain the results shown in Figure 12.5.

Figure 12.5   Log-likelihood functions for powers from WLS

```
MODEL:  MOD_1.

Source variable.. X                      Dependent variable.. Y

Log-likelihood Function =  -61.826560    POWER value =    .000
Log-likelihood Function =  -60.591503    POWER value =    .200
Log-likelihood Function =  -59.385889    POWER value =    .400
Log-likelihood Function =  -58.220191    POWER value =    .600
Log-likelihood Function =  -57.108016    POWER value =    .800
Log-likelihood Function =  -56.066817    POWER value =   1.000
Log-likelihood Function =  -55.118623    POWER value =   1.200
Log-likelihood Function =  -54.290631    POWER value =   1.400
Log-likelihood Function =  -53.615443    POWER value =   1.600
Log-likelihood Function =  -53.130626    POWER value =   1.800
Log-likelihood Function =  -52.877225    POWER value =   2.000
Log-likelihood Function =  -52.896965    POWER value =   2.200
Log-likelihood Function =  -53.228140    POWER value =   2.400
Log-likelihood Function =  -53.900705    POWER value =   2.600
Log-likelihood Function =  -54.931654    POWER value =   2.800
Log-likelihood Function =  -56.322024    POWER value =   3.000


The Value of POWER Maximizing Log-likelihood Function =  2.000
```

The largest value of the log-likelihood is for a power of 2, confirming our observation that the variance is related to the square of *x*.

The WLS Solutions

Figure 12.6 shows the WLS solution when the value of 2 is used for power.

Figure 12.6   Statistics for the best power value

```
Source variable..    X               POWER value =  2.000

Dependent variable.. Y

Listwise Deletion of Missing Data

Multiple R          .97387
R Square            .94842
Adjusted R Square   .94685
Standard Error      .17292

            Analysis of Variance:

            DF   SUM OF SQUARES     MEAN SQUARE

REGRESSION   1        18.143075       18.143075
RESIDUALS   33          .986776         .029902

F =    606.74502     Signif F =  .0000

----------------- Variables in the Equation ------------------

Variable          B        SE B      Beta        T   Sig T

X          1.130362     .045890   .973867   24.632   .0000
(Constant) -.580006     .189983            -3.053   .0045

Log-likelihood Function =  -52.877225


The following new variables are being created:

  Name        Label

  WGT#1       Weight for Y from WLS, MOD_1  X** -2.000
```

(The weights that are saved from the procedure are the reciprocals of x^2). You will note that, compared to the OLS results in Figure 12.2, the parameter estimates for the slope and intercept have not changed much. What has changed are their standard deviations. In the OLS solution, the standard deviation of the slope (*SE B*) is 0.086. In the WLS solution, the standard deviation of the slope is 0.046. Similarly, for the constant, the standard deviation has changed from 0.68 to 0.19.

Diagnostics from the Linear Regression Procedure

The Weight Estimation procedure will only estimate weights and provide summary regression statistics. You must use the Linear Regression procedure specifying the weight variable to obtain residuals and other diagnostic information. In fact, if you know the weights, there is no need to run the Weight Estimation procedure; you can perform weighted least-squares analyses using the Linear Regression procedure.

Draper and Smith estimated the weights for the example data by computing variances for cases with similar values of the independent variables. They then developed a quadratic regression model to predict the variances from the values of the independent variable. If you apply their weights using the Linear Regression procedure, you will obtain the summary statistics shown in Figure 12.7.

Figure 12.7   Summary statistics from the Draper and Smith estimated weights

```
Multiple R            .95975
R Square              .92111
Adjusted R Square     .91872
Standard Error       1.13577

Analysis of Variance
                    DF      Sum of Squares      Mean Square
Regression           1           497.04422        497.04422
Residual            33            42.56923          1.28998

F =     385.31256      Signif F =  .0000


----------------- Variables in the Equation -----------------

Variable            B        SE B       Beta       T   Sig T

X             1.164999    .059350    .959746    19.629  .0000
(Constant)    -.888995    .300037              -2.963  .0056


End Block Number    1    All requested variables entered.


NOTE: No plots will be produced when /REGWGT is specified.  You can SAVE the
appropriate variables and use other procedures (e.g.  EXAMINE and PLOT) to
produce the requested plots.  To plot weighted versions of the residuals and
predicted values, use COMPUTE before plotting:
COMPUTE RESID = SQRT(REGWGTvar) * RESID
COMPUTE PRED = SQRT(REGWGTvar) * PRED


From Equation    1:   2 new variables have been created.

    Name       Contents
    ----       --------

    PRE_2      Predicted Value
    RES_2      Residual
```

Note that the slope has changed somewhat from the OLS solution, as has the constant.

This solution also differs from that shown in Figure 12.6. One of the reasons for this difference is that Draper and Smith's weights are not as extreme as those estimated by the WLS procedure using a quadratic source model. Our estimated weights range from 0.75 to 0.0076, while Draper and Smith's range from 0.30 to 7.8. (The actual numbers used for the weights don't matter. All that matters is the proportionality.) The Draper and Smith weights are probably more realistic, since our estimated hundred-fold increase in variance over the observed range of the independent variable is probably too extreme.

To see how well the Draper and Smith WLS solution performs, let's examine the residuals. You must save the residuals and predicted values from the Linear Regression procedure, but you must transform them before plotting. They must be multiplied by the square root of the weight variable.

Figure 12.8 is a plot of the transformed residuals and predicted values.

Figure 12.8   Plot of transformed residuals and predicted values

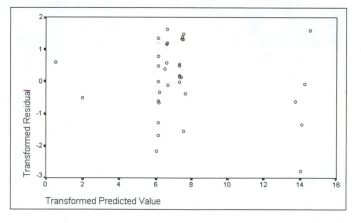

You see that the funnel shape that was evident in Figure 12.3 is no longer as marked. It appears that the WLS solution was successful.

13

Two-Stage Least-Squares Regression Examples

Macroeconomic data—data describing the overall state of the economy—frequently take the form of time series. Because of the complex interrelationships among macroeconomic variables, models for such data are usually afflicted with correlated errors: the errors in the equation are correlated with one or more of the predictor variables. When this is true, estimates made with ordinary least-squares (OLS) regression are biased. In this chapter, we will see how to use the technique known as two-stage least squares to deal with correlated errors using a classic macroeconomic model in a very modest setting.

The Artichoke Data

To illustrate the concepts involved in two-stage least squares, we will use a hypothetical set of data on the production of artichokes from Kelejian and Oates (1989). Three main series are involved in the model: the *demand* for artichokes, expressed as the quantity sold, in tons; the *price* of an artichoke in cents; and the average family *income* in thousands of dollars.

Figure 13.1 Demand, price, and income

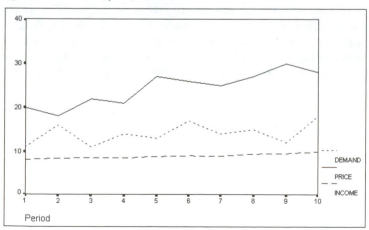

The Demand-Price-Income Economic Model

A classic economic model of the demand for some commodity, such as artichokes, is expressed as the following:

$$\text{DEMAND} = \beta_0 + \beta_1 \times \text{PRICE} + \beta_2 \times \text{INCOME} + \text{Error}$$

Equation 13.1

The path diagram shown in Figure 13.2 represents this equation.

Figure 13.2   Path diagram for simple model

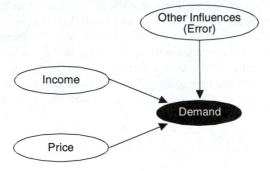

Although there is more to the model than this one equation, let's go ahead and estimate the coefficients using ordinary least-squares regression.

Estimation with Ordinary Least Squares

Figure 13.3 shows an ordinary least-squares (OLS) estimation of the model in Equation 13.1. This model estimates that an extra thousand dollars of mean family income increases the demand for artichokes by about 6.2 tons, while each extra penny in the price of artichokes decreases the demand by about 0.66 tons. Since Kelejian and Oates's data are hypothetical, we will not dwell on the interpretation of the coefficients. Instead, let us consider some difficulties with models such as the one in Equation 13.1.

Figure 13.3   OLS estimation of artichoke production

```
* * * *   M U L T I P L E   R E G R E S S I O N   * * * *

Listwise Deletion of Missing Data

Equation Number 1     Dependent Variable..   DEMAND

Block Number  1.  Method:  Enter     PRICE     INCOME


Variable(s) Entered on Step Number  1..     INCOME
                                    2..     PRICE


Multiple R          .73832     Analysis of Variance
R Square            .54512                     DF    Sum of Squares    Mean Square
Adjusted R Square   .41516     Regression       2        28.83688       14.41844
Standard Error     1.85407     Residual         7        24.06312        3.43759

                               F =      4.19435      Signif F =  .0635


----------------- Variables in the Equation -----------------

Variable            B        SE B       Beta        T   Sig T

PRICE         -.658904    .316896  -1.065767   -2.079   .0762
INCOME        6.208855   2.212209   1.438609    2.807   .0263
(Constant)  -25.081550  13.550746             -1.851   .1066


End Block Number   1   All requested variables entered.
```

Feedback and Correlated Errors

The difficulty with a model relating production, price, and income is that the influences work in both directions. Equation 13.1 states that the quantity of artichokes produced depends upon the price—when prices are high, farmers tend to grow more artichokes. It is equally true that the price depends upon production—a glut of artichokes on the market will force prices back down. (The model assumes that, at the market price, the demand for artichokes equals supply.) Thus, we should regard Equation 13.1 as part of a system of interrelated equations. The OLS solution shown above ignored the feedback effect of production on price. The real situation is more like the one shown in Figure 13.4.

Figure 13.4   Path diagram showing feedback

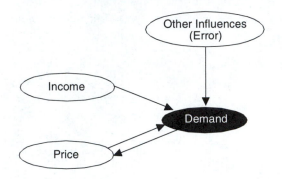

Suppose that something not included in the model (a new fertilizer, perhaps) leads to an increased quantity of artichokes on the market. Prices will fall due to the increased production. Because of the feedback relationship, high values of the error term in Figure 13.4 (which represents the effect of things not included in the equation) would be associated with low prices of artichokes.

Correlation of the error term with one of the predictor variables violates one of the assumptions of regression analysis. It leads to biased coefficients because the model in Figure 13.2 implies that price levels cause increased production. The OLS algorithm used by the Linear Regression procedure treats that portion of the error that is correlated with *price* as being caused by *price*—although really the correlation arises in the other direction, from the feedback effect of *demand* on *price*.

Note that it is the *theoretical* errors that are correlated with the predictor *price*. If you actually use the Linear Regression procedure, the OLS algorithm assumes the errors to be uncorrelated with the predictors and calculates biased coefficients in such a way as to produce uncorrelated residuals. Thus, you cannot use the estimated errors produced by a regression procedure to *check* for the problem of correlated errors. You know the correlated errors are there because of the feedback loop in the correctly specified model.

Two-Stage Least Squares

We know there are problems with the ordinary least-squares analysis presented above. The feedback relationship from the dependent variable *demand* to the predictor variable *price* produces correlations between the error term in Equation 13.1 and *price*, and therefore the estimates from OLS regression are biased.

Two-stage least squares (2SLS) is an important regression technique for models in which one (or more) of the predictor variables is thought to be correlated with the error term. Before we discuss 2SLS strategy, we need to introduce some terminology.

Endogenous Variables. Endogenous literally means *produced from within.* In regression analysis, an endogenous variable is a variable that is causally dependent on the other variable(s) in the model. When you are specifying models that solve several equations simultaneously (whether or not you explicitly solve all the equations), you know that several endogenous variables are present.

In a feedback situation, each of the variables in the feedback relationship is endogenous. Thus, in the model of Equation 13.1, *price* and *demand* are endogenous variables. The model should include the two-way relationship between *price* and *demand*, as in Figure 13.4.

Instruments. Instrumental variables, or simply *instruments,* are variables that are not influenced by other variables in the model but that do influence those variables. They may or may not be a part of the equation you are interested in, but they must be free of causal influence from any of the variables in that equation. To be effective, instruments should be:

- Highly correlated with the endogenous variables.
- Not correlated with the error terms.

A third, practical consideration is that the instrumental variables must be available for use in your analysis.

In Figure 13.5, you can see that there is a path *from* the instruments to the endogenous variable *price*, but that no paths lead *to* the instruments from the rest of the model.

Figure 13.5   Instrument variables

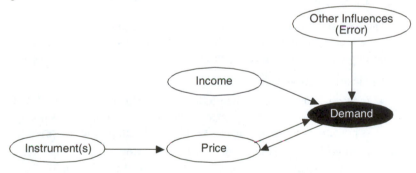

In practice, it is difficult to be sure whether an instrument is correlated with the (unobserved) error term. As noted in "Feedback and Correlated Errors" on p. 111, you cannot test this by using the estimated error terms from the Linear Regression procedure. When no instrument is readily available, the lagged value of the endogenous variable is often used. Even if this is correlated with the lagged error, it may not be correlated with the current error.

Strategy

In two-stage least squares, you are faced with a situation where an endogenous predictor variable (*price*) is correlated with the theoretical error terms in your model for the dependent variable (*demand*). OLS wrongly attributes some of the theoretically unexplained variation in *demand* to the effect of *price* because of this correlation. The 2SLS strategy is to replace the troublesome endogenous predictor variable *price* with a similar variable that:

- Is almost as good as *price* at predicting *demand*.
- Is not correlated with the theoretical error term in the prediction of *demand*.

You obtain such a replacement variable by ordinary regression, using the instruments to predict the endogenous variable. If the instruments have the two properties listed in "Two-Stage Least Squares" on p. 112, the predicted value of the endogenous variable will be:

- A good predictor of the dependent variable.
- Uncorrelated with the error term for the dependent variable.

To appreciate what is involved in two-stage least squares, we will work through the very simple demand-for-artichokes example using the Linear Regression procedure (in two stages). We will then see how the 2-Stage Least Squares procedure automates the process.

Stage 1: Estimating Price

The first stage requires instruments with which to predict *price*. If the instruments are not affected by *demand*, then the predicted values of *price* will likewise be unaffected by *demand* and we can safely use those predicted values in the second stage.

The instruments we will use are:

- *income*. This is one of the predictor variables in Equation 13.1. It is unlikely that the demand for artichokes affects the income of consumers in any large way, but it is possible that income levels will be useful in predicting price levels.
- *rainfall*. This variable is not a part of Equation 13.1 because we do not expect it to be useful in predicting the demand for artichokes. It should affect the price of artichokes, however, because of its effect on the quantity available. Since it is unlikely to be influenced by demand (or anything else), it is a suitable instrument.
- Lagged *price*. The lagged value of an endogenous variable is very often used as an instrument because it is frequently a good predictor of the current value. You have good reason to believe that the current demand for artichokes does not affect last season's price, so lagged price should be uncorrelated with the errors in the demand model.

The first stage of the estimation, using these instruments, is shown in Figure 13.6. The predicted values of *price* from this equation are saved in a new series named *pre_1*.

Figure 13.6   Using instruments to predict price

```
* * * *   M U L T I P L E   R E G R E S S I O N   * * * *

Listwise Deletion of Missing Data

Equation Number 1    Dependent Variable..   PRICE

Block Number  1.  Method: Enter    INCOME   RAINFALL LAGPRICE


Variable(s) Entered on Step Number  1..    LAGPRICE  LAGS(PRICE,1) on 29 Apr 93 at 15:34
                                    2..    RAINFALL
                                    3..    INCOME


Multiple R              .91854      Analysis of Variance
R Square                .84372                     DF    Sum of Squares    Mean Square
Adjusted R Square       .74996      Regression      3          98.62173       32.87391
Standard Error         1.91140      Residual        5          18.26716        3.65343

                                    F =      8.99809    Signif F =  .0185


----------------- Variables in the Equation ------------------

Variable             B          SE B        Beta        T    Sig T

INCOME         3.752000    2.994052      .506352    1.253   .2656
RAINFALL       -.217927     .105674     -.442332   -2.062   .0942
LAGPRICE        .418053     .417602      .430582    1.001   .3627
(Constant)    -8.579676   20.892358                 -.411   .6983


End Block Number   1   All requested variables entered.


        * * * *   M U L T I P L E   R E G R E S S I O N   * * * *

Equation Number 1    Dependent Variable..   PRICE


Residuals Statistics:

            Min      Max     Mean    Std Dev   N

*PRED     18.6584  29.8526  24.8889   3.5111   9
*RESID    -1.7745   2.7180    .0000   1.5111   9
*ZPRED    -1.7745   1.4137    .0000   1.0000   9
*ZRESID    -.9284   1.4220    .0000    .7906   9

Total Cases =       10



        * * * * * * * * * * * * * * * * * * * * * * * * * * * * *


From Equation   1:   1 new variables have been created.

  Name       Contents
  ----       --------

  PRE_1      Predicted Value
```

Stage 2: Estimating the Model

The second stage is to estimate the model we are interested in (Equation 13.1) with *pre_1* substituted for *price*. Figure 13.7 shows this procedure.

The regression coefficients in Figure 13.7 are the ones we want—the ones that belong in Equation 13.1, given what we know about feedback in the overall model. The coefficient of *income* is 9.561, and the coefficient of *price* is –1.265. Notice that both coefficients have changed appreciably from Figure 13.3, where we used ordinary least squares to estimate them.

Figure 13.7   Using pre_1 to predict demand

```
                    * * * *   M U L T I P L E   R E G R E S S I O N   * * * *

Listwise Deletion of Missing Data

Equation Number 1     Dependent Variable..   DEMAND

Block Number  1.  Method: Enter      PRE_1 INCOME


Variable(s) Entered on Step Number 1..    INCOME
                                   2..    PRE_1  Predicted Value


Multiple R            .85655        Analysis of Variance
R Square              .73368                        DF      Sum of Squares      Mean Square
Adjusted R Square     .64490        Regression       2           30.97742         15.48871
Standard Error       1.36899        Residual         6           11.24480          1.87413

                                    F =      8.26446      Signif F =  .0189


----------------- Variables in the Equation ------------------

Variable           B          SE B       Beta        T  Sig T

PRE_1        -1.265008      .345830  -1.933343    -3.658  .0106
INCOME        9.561323     2.353817   2.146960     4.062  .0066
(Constant)  -40.016582    13.708401              -2.919  .0267

End Block Number   1   All requested variables entered.
```

However, the R^2 and the standard errors reported in Figure 13.7 are not the ones we want. This is because Figure 13.7 shows an equation with *pre_1*, but we want the R^2 and standard errors for Equation 13.1, which uses *price*. The regression coefficients for the two equations are the same, but the R^2 and the standard errors are not. In order to obtain the correct standard errors, you must run the 2-Stage Least Squares procedure.

The 2-Stage Least Squares Procedure

Figure 13.8 shows the 2-Stage Least Squares results, without going through the two stages outlined above.

Figure 13.8   2-Stage Least Squares output

```
MODEL:  MOD_1.

Equation number:    1

Dependent variable.. DEMAND

Listwise Deletion of Missing Data

Multiple R             .68121
R Square               .46405
Adjusted R Square      .28540
Standard Error        2.44189


                 Analysis of Variance:

              DF    Sum of Squares      Mean Square
Regression     2         30.977420        15.488710
Residuals      6         35.776864         5.962811

F =       2.59755        Signif F =   .1539

Equation number:    1

Dependent variable.. DEMAND


----------------- Variables in the Equation -----------------

Variable              B        SE B       Beta        T  Sig T

PRICE          -1.265008     .616862  -2.104793   -2.051  .0862
INCOME          9.561323    4.198536   2.146960    2.277  .0630
(Constant)    -40.016582   24.451868              -1.637  .1528


Correlation Matrix of Parameter Estimates

                 PRICE        INCOME
PRICE        1.0000000     -.9171194
INCOME        -.9171194     1.0000000

The following new variables are being created:

   Name         Label

   FIT_1        Fit for DEMAND from 2SLS, MOD_1 Equation 1
   ERR_1        Error for DEMAND from 2SLS, MOD_1 Equation 1
```

The 2-Stage Least Squares procedure gives you the same results as two stages of OLS, with much less effort. The contrast in effort required is even more striking in larger models.

The 2-Stage Least Squares procedure is quite simple to specify. You must, however, understand the model you are estimating if you are to specify it correctly.

Syntax Reference

Introduction

This syntax reference guide describes the SPSS command language underlying SPSS Regression Models. Most of the features of these commands are implemented in the dialog boxes; you can use those features directly from the dialog boxes or paste the syntax into a syntax window and edit it to include additional specifications or to build a command file that you can save and reuse. Other features are available only in command syntax. For more information about SPSS command syntax, see Universals in the *SPSS Base Syntax Reference Guide*. For more information about running commands in SPSS, see the *SPSS Base User's Guide*.

A Few Useful Terms

All terms in the SPSS command language fall into one or more of the following categories:

- **Keyword**. A word already defined by SPSS to identify a command, subcommand, or specification. Most keywords are, or resemble, common English words.
- **Command**. A specific instruction that controls the execution of SPSS.
- **Subcommand**. Additional instructions for SPSS commands. A command can contain more than one subcommand, each with its own specifications.
- **Specifications**. Instructions added to a command or subcommand. Specifications may include subcommands, keywords, numbers, arithmetic operators, variable names, special delimiters, and so forth.

Each command begins with a command keyword (which may contain more than one word). The command keyword is followed by at least one blank space and then any additional specifications. Each command ends with a command terminator, which is usually a period. For example:

Syntax Diagrams

Each SPSS command described in this manual includes a syntax diagram that shows all of the subcommands, keywords, and specifications allowed for that command. By remembering the following rules, you can use the syntax diagram as a quick reference for any command.

- Elements shown in all capital letters are keywords defined by SPSS to identify commands, subcommands, functions, operators, and other specifications.
- Elements in lower case describe specifications you supply.

- Elements in boldface type are defaults. A default indicated with ** is in effect when the keyword is not specified.
- Parentheses, apostrophes, and quotation marks are required where indicated.
- Elements enclosed in square brackets ([ ]) are optional.
- Braces ({ }) indicate a choice between elements. You can specify any one of the elements enclosed within the aligned braces.
- Ellipses indicate that an element can be repeated.
- Most abbreviations are obvious; for example, varname stands for variable name and varlist stands for a list of variables.
- The command terminator is not shown in the syntax diagrams.

Syntax Rules

Keep in mind the following simple rules when editing and writing command syntax:

- Each command must begin on a new line and end with a period (.).
- Most subcommands are separated by slashes (/). The slash before the first subcommand on a command is usually optional.
- Variable names must be spelled out fully.
- Text included within apostrophes or quotation marks must be contained on a single line.
- Each line of command syntax cannot exceed 80 characters.
- A period (.) must be used to indicate decimals, regardless of any International settings on your computer.
- Variable names ending in a period can cause errors in commands created by the dialog boxes. You cannot create such variable names in the dialog boxes, and you should generally avoid them.

SPSS command syntax is case-insensitive, and three-letter abbreviations can be used for many command specifications. You can use as many lines as you want to specify a single command. You can add space or break lines at almost any point where a single blank is allowed, such as around slashes, parentheses, arithmetic operators, or between variable names. For example,

```
FREQUENCIES
 VARIABLES=JOBCAT SEXRACE
 /PERCENTILES=25 50 75
 /BARCHART.
```

and

```
freq var=jobcat sexrace /percent=25 50 75 /bar.
```

are both acceptable alternatives that generate the same results.

Batch Mode and INCLUDE Files

For SPSS command files run in batch mode (see the *SPSS Base User's Guide*) or via the SPSS INCLUDE command, the syntax rules are slightly different:

- Each command must begin in the first column of a new line.
- Continuation lines must be indented at least one space.
- The period at the end of the command is optional.

If you generate command syntax by pasting dialog box choices into a syntax window, the format of the commands is suitable for all modes of operation.

LOGISTIC REGRESSION

```
LOGISTIC REGRESSION [VARIABLES =] dependent var
        [WITH independent varlist [BY var [BY var] ... ]]

[/CATEGORICAL = var1, var2, ... ]

[/CONTRAST (categorical var) = [{INDICATOR [(refcat)]    }]]
                                {DEVIATION [(refcat)]    }
                                {SIMPLE [(refcat)]       }
                                {DIFFERENCE              }
                                {HELMERT                 }
                                {REPEATED                }
                                {POLYNOMIAL[({1,2,3...})]}
                                          {metric  }
                                {SPECIAL (matrix)        }

[/METHOD = {ENTER**        }    [{ALL      }]]
           {BSTEP [{COND}]}     {varlist}
                  {LR  }
                  {WALD}
           {FSTEP [{COND}]}
                  {LR  }
                  {WALD}

[/SELECT = {ALL**                     }]
           {varname relation value}

[/{NOORIGIN**}]
  {ORIGIN   }

[/ID = [variable]]

[/PRINT = [DEFAULT**] [SUMMARY] [CORR] [ALL] [ITER [({1})]] [GOODFIT]]
                                                   {n}
          [CI(level)]

[/CRITERIA = [BCON ({0.001**})] [ITERATE({20**})] [LCON({0.01**})]
                   {value }              {n  }         {value }

             [PIN({0.05**})] [POUT({0.10**})] [EPS({.00000001**})]]
                 {value }        {value }         {value       }

             [CUT[{0.5**  }]]
                 {value  }

[/CLASSPLOT]

[/MISSING = {EXCLUDE **}]
            {INCLUDE   }

[/CASEWISE = [tempvarlist]  [OUTLIER({2**  })]]
                                    {value}

[/SAVE = tempvar[(newname)] tempvar[(newname)]...]

[/EXTERNAL]
```

** Default if the subcommand or keyword is omitted.

Temporary variables created by LOGISTIC REGRESSION are:

PRED	LEVER	COOK
PGROUP	LRESID	DFBETA
RESID	SRESID	
DEV	ZRESID	

Example:

```
LOGISTIC REGRESSION PROMOTED WITH AGE, JOBTIME, JOBRATE.
```

Overview

LOGISTIC REGRESSION regresses a dichotomous dependent variable on a set of independent variables (Aldrich and Nelson, 1984; Fox, 1984; Hosmer and Lemeshow, 1989; McCullagh and Nelder, 1989; Agresti, 1990). Categorical independent variables are replaced by sets of contrast variables, each set entering and leaving the model in a single step.

Options

Processing of Independent Variables. You can specify which independent variables are categorical in nature on the CATEGORICAL subcommand. You can control treatment of categorical independent variables by the CONTRAST subcommand. Seven methods are available for entering independent variables into the model. You can specify any one of them on the METHOD subcommand. You can also use the keyword BY between variable names to enter interaction terms.

Selecting Cases. You can use the SELECT subcommand to define subsets of cases to be used in estimating a model.

Regression through the Origin. You can use the ORIGIN subcommand to exclude a constant term from a model.

Specifying Termination and Model-Building Criteria. You can further control computations when building the model by specifying criteria on the CRITERIA subcommand.

Adding New Variables to the Working Data File. You can save the residuals, predicted values, and diagnostics generated by LOGISTIC REGRESSION in the working data file.

Output. You can use the PRINT subcommand to print optional output, use the CASEWISE subcommand to request analysis of residuals, and use the ID subcommand to specify a variable whose values or value labels identify cases in output. You can request plots of the actual and predicted values for each case with the CLASSPLOT subcommand.

Basic Specification

- The minimum specification is the VARIABLES subcommand with one dichotomous dependent variable. You must specify a list of independent variables either following the keyword WITH on the VARIABLES subcommand or on a METHOD subcommand.

- The default output includes goodness-of-fit tests for the model (-2 log-likelihood, goodness-of-fit statistic, Cox and Snell R^2, and NagelKerke R^2) and a classification table for the predicted and observed group memberships. The regression coefficient, standard error of the regression coefficient, Wald statistic and its significance level, and a multiple correlation coefficient adjusted for the number of parameters (Atkinson, 1980) are displayed for each variable in the equation.

Subcommand Order

- Subcommands can be named in any order. If the VARIABLES subcommand is not specified first, a slash (/) must precede it.
- The ordering of METHOD subcommands determines the order in which models are estimated. Different sequences may result in different models.

Syntax Rules

- Only one dependent variable can be specified for each LOGISTIC REGRESSION.
- Any number of independent variables may be listed. The dependent variable may not appear on this list.
- The independent variable list is required if any of the METHOD subcommands are used without a variable list or if the METHOD subcommand is not used. The keyword TO cannot be used on any variable list.
- If you specify the keyword WITH on the VARIABLES subcommand, all independent variables must be listed.
- If the keyword WITH is used on the VARIABLES subcommand, interaction terms do not have to be specified on the variable list, but the individual variables that make up the interactions must be listed.
- Multiple METHOD subcommands are allowed.
- The minimum truncation for this command is LOGI REG.

Operations

- Independent variables specified on the CATEGORICAL subcommand are replaced by sets of contrast variables. In stepwise analyses, the set of contrast variables associated with a categorical variable is entered or removed from the model as a single step.
- Independent variables are screened to detect and eliminate redundancies.
- If the linearly dependent variable is one of a set of contrast variables, the set will be reduced by the redundant variable or variables. A warning will be issued, and the reduced set will be used.
- For the forward stepwise method, redundancy checking is done when a variable is to be entered into the model.
- When backward stepwise or direct-entry methods are requested, all variables for each METHOD subcommand are checked for redundancy before that analysis begins.

Limitations

- The dependent variable must be dichotomous for each split-file group. Specifying a dependent variable with more or less than two nonmissing values per split-file group will result in an error.

Example

```
LOGISTIC REGRESSION PASS WITH GPA, MAT, GRE.
```

- *PASS* is specified as the dependent variable.
- *GPA*, *MAT*, and *GRE* are specified as independent variables.
- LOGISTIC REGRESSION produces the default output for the logistic regression of *PASS* on *GPA*, *MAT*, and *GRE*.

VARIABLES Subcommand

VARIABLES specifies the dependent variable and, optionally, all independent variables in the model. The dependent variable appears first on the list and is separated from the independent variables by the keyword WITH.

- One VARIABLES subcommand is allowed for each Logistic Regression procedure.
- The dependent variable must be dichotomous—that is, it must have exactly two values other than system-missing and user-missing values for each split-file group.
- The dependent variable may be a string variable if its two values can be differentiated by their first eight characters.
- You can indicate an interaction term on the variable list by using the keyword BY to separate the individual variables.
- If all METHOD subcommands are accompanied by independent variable lists, the keyword WITH and the list of independent variables may be omitted.
- If the keyword WITH is used, *all* independent variables must be specified. For interaction terms, only the individual variable names that make up the interaction (for example, X1, X2) need to be specified. Specifying the actual interaction term (for example, X1 BY X2) on the VARIABLES subcommand is optional if you specify it on a METHOD subcommand.

Example

```
LOGISTIC REGRESSION PROMOTED WITH AGE,JOBTIME,JOBRATE,
    AGE BY JOBTIME.
```

- *PROMOTED* is specified as the dependent variable.
- *AGE*, *JOBTIME*, *JOBRATE*, and the interaction *AGE* by *JOBTIME* are specified as the independent variables.
- Because no METHOD is specified, all three single independent variables and the interaction term are entered into the model.
- LOGISTIC REGRESSION produces the default output.

CATEGORICAL Subcommand

CATEGORICAL identifies independent variables that are nominal or ordinal. Variables that are declared to be categorical are automatically transformed to a set of contrast variables as specified on the CONTRAST subcommand. If a variable coded as $0-1$ is declared as categorical, its coding scheme will be changed to deviation contrasts by default.

- Independent variables not specified on CATEGORICAL are assumed to be at least interval level, except for string variables.
- Any variable specified on CATEGORICAL is ignored if it does not appear either after WITH on the VARIABLES subcommand or on any METHOD subcommand.
- Variables specified on CATEGORICAL are replaced by sets of contrast variables. If the categorical variable has n distinct values, there will be $n-1$ contrast variables generated. The set of contrast variables associated with a categorical variable is entered or removed from the model as a step.
- If any one of the variables in an interaction term is specified on CATEGORICAL, the interaction term is replaced by contrast variables.
- All string variables are categorical. Only the first eight characters of each value of a string variable are used in distinguishing between values. Thus, if two values of a string variable are identical for the first eight characters, the values are treated as though they were the same.

Example

```
LOGISTIC REGRESSION PASS WITH GPA, GRE, MAT, CLASS, TEACHER
/CATEGORICAL = CLASS,TEACHER.
```

- The dichotomous dependent variable *PASS* is regressed on the interval-level independent variables *GPA*, *GRE*, and *MAT* and the categorical variables *CLASS* and *TEACHER*.

CONTRAST Subcommand

CONTRAST specifies the type of contrast used for categorical independent variables. The interpretation of the regression coefficients for categorical variables depends on the contrasts used. The default is INDICATOR. The categorical independent variable is specified in parentheses following CONTRAST. The closing parenthesis is followed by one of the contrast-type keywords.

- If the categorical variable has n values, there will be $n-1$ rows in the contrast matrix. Each contrast matrix is treated as a set of independent variables in the analysis.
- Only one categorical independent variable can be specified per CONTRAST subcommand, but multiple CONTRAST subcommands can be specified.

The following contrast types are available. See Finn (1974) and Kirk (1982) for further information on a specific type. For illustration of contrast types, see the appendix "Categorical Variable Coding Schemes."

INDICATOR(refcat)   *Indicator variables.* Contrasts indicate the presence or absence of category membership. By default, refcat is the last category (represented in the contrast matrix as a row of zeros). To omit a category other than the last, specify the sequence number of the omitted category (which is not necessarily the same as its value) in parentheses after the keyword INDICATOR.

DEVIATION(refcat)   *Deviations from the overall effect.* This is the default. The effect for each category of the independent variable except one is compared to the overall effect. Refcat is the category for which parameter estimates are not displayed (they must be calculated from the others). By default, refcat is the last category. To omit a category other than the last, specify the sequence number of the omitted category (which is not necessarily the same as its value) in parentheses after the keyword DEVIATION.

SIMPLE(refcat)   *Each category of the independent variable except the last is compared to the last category.* To use a category other than the last as the omitted reference category, specify its sequence number (which is not necessarily the same as its value) in parentheses following the keyword SIMPLE.

DIFFERENCE   *Difference or reverse Helmert contrasts.* The effects for each category of the independent variable except the first are compared to the mean effects of the previous categories.

HELMERT   *Helmert contrasts.* The effects for each category of the independent variable except the last are compared to the mean effects of subsequent categories.

POLYNOMIAL(metric)   *Polynomial contrasts.* The first degree of freedom contains the linear effect across the categories of the independent variable, the second contains the quadratic effect, and so on. By default, the categories are assumed to be equally spaced; unequal spacing can be specified by entering a metric consisting of one integer for each category of the independent variable in parentheses after the keyword POLYNOMIAL. For example, `CONTRAST(STIMULUS)=POLYNOMIAL(1,2,4)` indicates that the three levels of STIMULUS are actually in the proportion 1:2:4. The default metric is always $(1,2,...,k)$, where k categories are involved. Only the relative differences between the terms of the metric matter: $(1,2,4)$ is the same metric as $(2,3,5)$ or $(20,30,50)$ because the difference between the second and third numbers is twice the difference between the first and second in each instance.

REPEATED   *Comparison of adjacent categories.* Each category of the independent variable except the first is compared to the previous category.

SPECIAL(matrix)   *A user-defined contrast.* After this keyword, a matrix is entered in parentheses with $k - 1$ rows and k columns (where k is the number of categories of the independent variable). The rows of the contrast matrix contain the special contrasts indicating the desired comparisons between categories. If the special contrasts are linear combinations of each other, LOGISTIC REGRESSION reports the linear dependency and stops processing. If k rows are entered, the first row is discarded and only the last $k - 1$ rows are used as the contrast matrix in the analysis.

Example

```
LOGISTIC REGRESSION PASS WITH GRE, CLASS
 /CATEGORICAL = CLASS
 /CONTRAST(CLASS)=HELMERT.
```

- A logistic regression analysis of the dependent variable *PASS* is performed on the interval independent variable *GRE* and the categorical independent variable *CLASS*.

- *PASS* is a dichotomous variable representing course pass/fail status and *CLASS* identifies whether a student is in one of three classrooms. A HELMERT contrast is requested.

Example

```
LOGISTIC REGRESSION PASS WITH GRE, CLASS
 /CATEGORICAL = CLASS
 /CONTRAST(CLASS)=SPECIAL(2 -1 -1
                          0  1 -1).
```

- In this example, the contrasts are specified with the keyword SPECIAL.

METHOD Subcommand

METHOD indicates how the independent variables enter the model. The specification is the METHOD subcommand followed by a single method keyword. The keyword METHOD can be omitted. Optionally, specify the independent variables and interactions for which the method is to be used. Use the keyword BY between variable names of an interaction term.

- If no variable list is specified or if the keyword ALL is used, all of the independent variables following the keyword WITH on the VARIABLES subcommand are eligible for inclusion in the model.

- If no METHOD subcommand is specified, the default method is ENTER.

- Variables specified on CATEGORICAL are replaced by sets of contrast variables. The set of contrast variables associated with a categorical variable is entered or removed from the model as a single step.

- Any number of METHOD subcommands can appear in a Logistic Regression procedure. METHOD subcommands are processed in the order in which they are specified. Each method starts with the results from the previous method. If BSTEP is used, all remaining eligible variables are entered at the first step. All variables are then eligible for entry and removal unless they have been excluded from the METHOD variable list.

- The beginning model for the first METHOD subcommand is either the constant variable (by default or if NOORIGIN is specified) or an empty model (if ORIGIN is specified).

The available METHOD keywords are:

ENTER   *Forced entry.* All variables are entered in a single step. This is the default if the METHOD subcommand is omitted.

FSTEP   *Forward stepwise.* The variables (or interaction terms) specified on FSTEP are tested for entry into the model one by one, based on the significance level of the score statistic. The variable with the smallest significance less than PIN is entered into the model. After each entry, variables that are already in the model are tested for possible removal, based on the significance of the conditional statistic, the Wald statistic, or the likelihood-ratio criterion. The variable with the largest probability greater than the specified POUT value is removed and the model is reestimated. Variables in the model are then evaluated again for removal. Once no more variables satisfy the removal criterion, covariates not in the model are evaluated for entry. Model building stops when no more variables meet entry or removal criteria, or when the current model is the same as a previous one.

BSTEP   *Backward stepwise.* As a first step, the variables (or interaction terms) specified on BSTEP are entered into the model together and are tested for removal one by one. Stepwise removal and entry then follow the same process as described for FSTEP until no more variables meet entry or removal criteria, or when the current model is the same as a previous one.

The statistic used in the test for removal can be specified by an additional keyword in parentheses following FSTEP or BSTEP. If FSTEP or BSTEP is specified by itself, the default is COND.

COND   *Conditional statistic.* This is the default if FSTEP or BSTEP is specified by itself.

WALD   *Wald statistic.* The removal of a variable from the model is based on the significance of the Wald statistic.

LR   *Likelihood ratio.* The removal of a variable from the model is based on the significance of the change in the log-likelihood. If LR is specified, the model must be reestimated without each of the variables in the model. This can substantially increase computational time. However, the likelihood-ratio statistic is the best criterion for deciding which variables are to be removed.

Example

```
LOGISTIC REGRESSION PROMOTED WITH AGE JOBTIME JOBRATE RACE SEX AGENCY
 /CATEGORICAL RACE SEX AGENCY
 /METHOD ENTER AGE  JOBTIME
 /METHOD BSTEP (LR) RACE SEX JOBRATE AGENCY.
```

- *AGE*, *JOBTIME*, *JOBRATE*, *RACE*, *SEX*, and *AGENCY* are specified as independent variables. *RACE*, *SEX*, and *AGENCY* are specified as categorical independent variables.

- The first METHOD subcommand enters *AGE* and *JOBTIME* into the model.

- Variables in the model at the termination of the first METHOD subcommand are included in the model at the beginning of the second METHOD subcommand.

- The second METHOD subcommand adds the variables *RACE*, *SEX*, *JOBRATE*, and *AGENCY* to the previous model.

- Backward stepwise logistic regression analysis is then done with only the variables on the BSTEP variable list tested for removal using the LR statistic.

- The procedure continues until all variables from the BSTEP variable list have been removed or the removal of a variable will not result in a decrease in the log-likelihood with a probability larger than POUT.

SELECT Subcommand

By default, all cases in the working data file are considered for inclusion in LOGISTIC REGRESSION. Use the optional SELECT subcommand to include a subset of cases in the analysis.

- The specification is either a logical expression or keyword ALL. ALL is the default. Variables named on VARIABLES, CATEGORICAL, or METHOD subcommands cannot appear on SELECT.
- In the logical expression on SELECT, the relation can be EQ, NE, LT, LE, GT, or GE. The variable must be numeric and the value can be any number.
- Only cases for which the logical expression on SELECT is true are included in calculations. All other cases, including those with missing values for the variable named on SELECT, are unselected.
- Diagnostic statistics and classification statistics are reported for both selected and unselected cases.
- Cases deleted from the working data file with the SELECT IF or SAMPLE command are not included among either the selected or unselected cases.

Example

```
LOGISTIC REGRESSION VARIABLES=GRADE WITH GPA,TUCE,PSI
 /SELECT SEX EQ 1 /CASEWISE=RESID.
```

- Only cases with the value 1 for *SEX* are included in the logistic regression analysis.
- Residual values generated by CASEWISE are displayed for both selected and unselected cases.

ORIGIN and NOORIGIN Subcommands

ORIGIN and NOORIGIN control whether or not the constant is included. NOORIGIN (the default) includes a constant term (intercept) in all equations. ORIGIN suppresses the constant term and requests regression through the origin. (NOCONST can be used as an alias for ORIGIN.)

- The only specification is either ORIGIN or NOORIGIN.
- ORIGIN or NOORIGIN can be specified only once per Logistic Regression procedure, and it affects all METHOD subcommands.

Example

```
LOGISTIC REGRESSION VARIABLES=PASS WITH GPA,GRE,MAT /ORIGIN.
```

- ORIGIN suppresses the automatic generation of a constant term.

ID Subcommand

ID specifies a variable whose values or value labels identify the casewise listing. By default, cases are labeled by their case number.

- The only specification is the name of a single variable that exists in the working data file.

- Only the first eight characters of the variable's value labels are used to label cases. If the variable has no value labels, the values are used.
- Only the first eight characters of a string variable are used to label cases.

PRINT Subcommand

PRINT controls the display of optional output. If PRINT is omitted, DEFAULT output (defined below) is displayed.

- The minimum specification is PRINT followed by a single keyword.
- If PRINT is used, only the requested output is displayed.

DEFAULT	*Goodness-of-fit tests for the model, classification tables, and statistics for the variables in and not in the equation at each step.* Tables and statistics are displayed for each split file and METHOD subcommand.
SUMMARY	*Summary information.* Same output as DEFAULT, except that the output for each step is not displayed.
CORR	*Correlation matrix of parameter estimates for the variables in the model.*
ITER(value)	*Iterations at which parameter estimates are to be displayed.* The value in parentheses controls the spacing of iteration reports. If the value is n, the parameter estimates are displayed for every nth iteration starting at 0. If a value is not supplied, intermediate estimates are displayed at each iteration.
GOODFIT	*Hosmer-Lemeshow goodness-of-fit statistic* (Hosmer and Lemeshow, 1989).
CI(level)	*Confidence interval for exp(B).* The value in parentheses must be an integer between 1 and 99.
ALL	*All available output.*

Example

```
LOGISTIC REGRESSION VARIABLES=PASS WITH GPA,GRE,MAT
 /METHOD FSTEP
 /PRINT CORR SUMMARY ITER(2).
```

- A forward stepwise logistic regression analysis of *PASS* on *GPA*, *GRE*, and *MAT* is specified.
- The PRINT subcommand requests the display of the correlation matrix of parameter estimates for the variables in the model (CORR), classification tables and statistics for the variables in and not in the equation for the final model (SUMMARY), and parameter estimates at every second iteration (ITER(2)).

CRITERIA Subcommand

CRITERIA controls the statistical criteria used in building the logistic regression models. The way in which these criteria are used depends on the method specified on the METHOD subcommand. The default criteria are noted in the description of each keyword below. Iterations will stop if the criterion for BCON, LCON, or ITERATE is satisfied.

BCON(value) *Change in parameter estimates to terminate iteration.* Iteration terminates when the parameters change by less than the specified value. The default is 0.001. To eliminate this criterion, specify a value of 0.

ITERATE *Maximum number of iterations.* The default is 20.

LCON(value) *Percentage change in the log-likelihood ratio for termination of iterations.* If the log-likelihood decreases by less than the specified value, iteration terminates. The default is 0.01. To eliminate this criterion, specify a value of 0.

PIN(value) *Probability of score statistic for variable entry.* The default is 0.05. The larger the specified probability, the easier it is for a variable to enter the model.

POUT(value) *Probability of conditional, Wald, or LR statistic to remove a variable.* The default is 0.1. The larger the specified probability, the easier it is for a variable to remain in the model.

EPS(value) *Epsilon value used for redundancy checking.* The specified value must be less than or equal to 0.05 and greater than or equal to 10^{-12}. The default is 10^{-8}. Larger values make it harder for variables to pass the redundancy check—that is, they are more likely to be removed from the analysis.

CUT(value) *Cutoff value for classification.* A case is assigned to a group when the predicted event probability is greater than or equal to the cutoff value. The cutoff value affects the value of the dichotomous derived variable in the classification table, the predicted group (PGROUP on CASEWISE), and the classification plot (CLASSPLOT). The default cutoff value is 0.5. You can specify a value between 0 and 1 (0 < value < 1).

Example

```
LOGISTIC REGRESSION PROMOTED WITH AGE JOBTIME RACE
 /CATEGORICAL RACE
 /METHOD BSTEP
 /CRITERIA BCON(0.01) PIN(0.01) POUT(0.05).
```

- A backward stepwise logistic regression analysis is performed for the dependent variable *PROMOTED* and the independent variables *AGE*, *JOBTIME*, and *RACE*.
- CRITERIA alters four of the statistical criteria that control the building of a model.
- BCON specifies that if the change in the absolute value of all of the parameter estimates is less than 0.01, the iterative estimation process should stop. Larger values lower the number of iterations required. Notice that the ITER and LCON criteria remain unchanged and that if either of them is met before BCON, iterations will terminate. (LCON can be set to 0 if only BCON and ITER are to be used.)
- POUT requires that the probability of the statistic used to test whether a variable should remain in the model be smaller than 0.05. This is more stringent than the default value of 0.1.
- PIN requires that the probability of the score statistic used to test whether a variable should be included be smaller than 0.01. This makes it more difficult for variables to be included in the model than the default value of 0.05.

CLASSPLOT Subcommand

CLASSPLOT generates a classification plot of the actual and predicted values of the dichotomous dependent variable at each step.

- Keyword CLASSPLOT is the only specification.
- If CLASSPLOT is not specified, plots are not generated.

Example

```
LOGISTIC REGRESSION PROMOTED WITH JOBTIME RACE
 /CATEGORICAL RACE
 /CLASSPLOT.
```

- A logistic regression model is constructed for the dichotomous dependent variable *PROMOTED* and the independent variables *JOBTIME* and *RACE*.
- CLASSPLOT produces a classification plot for the dependent variable *PROMOTED*. The vertical axis of the plot is the frequency of the variable *PROMOTED*. The horizontal axis is the predicted probability of membership in the second of the two levels of *PROMOTED*.

CASEWISE Subcommand

CASEWISE produces a casewise listing of the values of the temporary variables created by LOGISTIC REGRESSION.

The following keywords are available for specifying temporary variables (see Fox, 1984). When CASEWISE is specified by itself, the default lists *PRED*, *PGROUP*, *RESID*, and *ZRESID*. If a list of variable names is given, only those named temporary variables are displayed.

PRED　　*Predicted probability.* For each case, the predicted probability of having the second of the two values of the dichotomous dependent variable.

PGROUP　　*Predicted group.* The group to which a case is assigned based on the predicted probability.

RESID　　*Difference between observed and predicted probabilities.*

DEV　　*Deviance values.* For each case, a log-likelihood-ratio statistic, which measures how well the model fits the case, is computed.

LRESID　　*Logit residual.* Residual divided by the product of *PRED* and $1-$šš*PRED*.

SRESID　　*Studentized residual.*

ZRESID　　*Normalized residual.* Residual divided by the square root of the product of *PRED* and $1-$šš*PRED*.

LEVER　　*Leverage value.* A measure of the relative influence of each observation on the model's fit.

COOK　　*Analog of Cook's influence statistic.*

DFBETA　　*Difference in beta.* The difference in the estimated coefficients for each independent variable if the case is omitted.

The following keyword is available for restricting the cases to be displayed, based on the absolute value of *SRESID*:

OUTLIER (value)   *Cases with absolute values of SRESID greater than or equal to the specified value are displayed.* If OUTLIER is specified with no value, the default is 2.

Example

```
LOGISTIC REGRESSION PROMOTED WITH JOBTIME SEX RACE
 /CATEGORICAL SEX RACE
 /METHOD ENTER
 /CASEWISE SRESID LEVER DFBETA.
```

- CASEWISE produces a casewise listing of the temporary variables *SRESID*, *LEVER*, and *DFBETA*.
- There will be one *DFBETA* value for each parameter in the model. The continuous variable *JOBTIME*, the two-level categorical variable *SEX*, and the constant each require one parameter while the four-level categorical variable *RACE* requires three parameters. Thus, six values of *DFBETA* will be produced for each case.

MISSING Subcommand

LOGISTIC REGRESSION excludes all cases with missing values on any of the independent variables. For a case with a missing value on the dependent variable, predicted values are calculated if it has nonmissing values on all independent variables. The MISSING subcommand controls the processing of user-missing values. If the subcommand is not specified, the default is EXCLUDE.

EXCLUDE   *Delete cases with user-missing values as well as system-missing values.* This is the default.

INCLUDE   *Include user-missing values in the analysis.*

SAVE Subcommand

SAVE saves the temporary variables created by LOGISTIC REGRESSION. To specify variable names for the new variables, assign the new names in parentheses following each temporary variable name. If new variable names are not specified, LOGISTIC REGRESSION generates default names.

- Assigned variable names must be unique in the working data file. Scratch or system variable names (that is, names that begin with # or $) cannot be used.
- A temporary variable can be saved only once on the same SAVE subcommand.

Example

```
LOGISTIC REGRESSION PROMOTED WITH JOBTIME AGE
 /SAVE PRED (PREDPRO) DFBETA (DF).
```

- A logistic regression analysis of *PROMOTED* on the independent variables *JOBTIME* and *AGE* is performed.
- SAVE adds four variables to the working data file: one variable named *PREDPRO*, containing the predicted value from the specified model for each case, and three variables named *DF0*, *DF1*, and *DF2*, containing, respectively, the *DFBETA* values for each case of the constant, the independent variable *JOBTIME*, and the independent variable *AGE*.

EXTERNAL Subcommand

EXTERNAL indicates that the data for each split-file group should be held in an external scratch file during processing. This can help conserve memory resources when running complex analyses or analyses with large data sets.

- The keyword EXTERNAL is the only specification.
- Specifying EXTERNAL may result in slightly longer processing time.
- If EXTERNAL is not specified, all data are held internally and no scratch file is written.

NOMREG

```
NOMREG dependent varname [BY factor list] [WITH covariate list]

[/CRITERIA = [CIN({95**})] [DELTA({0**})] [MXITER({100**})] [MXSTEP({5**})]
             {n  }        {n  }          {n   }           {n  }
             [LCONVERGE({0**})] [PCONVERGE({1.0E-6**})] [SINGULAR({1E-8**})]
                       {n  }              {n      }             {n    }

[/FULLFACTORIAL]

[/INTERCEPT = {EXCLUDE   }]
             {INCLUDE**}

[/MISSING = {EXCLUDE**}]
           {INCLUDE  }

[/MODEL = {[effect effect ...]}]

[/PRINT = [CELLPROB] [CLASSTABLE] [CORB] [HISTORY({1**})]]]
          [SUMMARY ] [PARAMETER ] [COVB] [FIT] [LRT]
                                                {n  }

[/SCALE = {1**     }]
          {n      }
          {DEVIANCE}
          {PEARSON }

[/SUBPOP = varlist]

[/TEST[(valuelist)] = {['label'] effect valuelist effect valuelist...;}]
                      {['label'] ALL list;                           }
                      {['label'] ALL list                            }
```

**The default value.

Overview

NOMREG is a procedure for fitting a multinomial logit model to a polytomous nominal dependent variable.

Options

Tuning the algorithm. You can control the values of algorithm-tuning parameters with the CRITERIA subcommand.

Optional output. You can request additional output through the PRINT subcommand.

Basic Specification

The basic specification is one dependent variable.

Syntax Rules

- Minimum syntax—at least one dependent variable must be specified.
- The variable specification must come first.
- Subcommands can be specified in any order.
- Empty subcommands except the MODEL subcommand are ignored.
- The MODEL and the FULLFACTORIAL subcommands are mutually exclusive. Only one of them can be specified at any time.
- When repeated subcommands except the TEST subcommand are specified, all specifications except the last valid one are discarded.
- The following words are reserved as keywords or internal commands in the NOMREG procedure: BY, WITH, WITHIN.

Variable List

The variable list specifies the dependent variable and the factors in the model.
- The dependent variable must be the first specification on NOMREG. It can be of any type (numeric or string). Values of the dependent variable are sorted in ascending order. The lowest value defines the first category, and the highest value defines the last category.
- Factor variables can be of any type (numeric or string). The factors follow the dependent variable separated by the keyword BY.
- Covariate variables must be numeric. The covariates follow the factors, separated by the keyword WITH.
- If the WEIGHT command is specified, then the weight values are used as frequency counts for the respective category combination. Also, positive fractional weight values are rounded to the nearest integral value.

CRITERIA Subcommand

The CRITERIA subcommand offers controls on the iterative algorithm used for estimation and specifies numerical tolerance for checking singularity.

CIN(n)   *Confidence interval level.* Specify a value greater than or equal to 0 and less than 100. The default value is 95.

DELTA(n)   *Delta value added to observed cell frequency.* Specify a nonnegative value less than 1. The default value is 0.

LCONVERGE(n)   *Log-likelihood function convergence criterion.* Convergence is assumed if the absolute change or relative change in the log-likelihood function is less than this value. The criterion is not used if the value is 0. Specify a nonnegative value. The default value is 0.

MXITER(n)   *Maximum number of iterations.* Specify a positive integer. The default value is 100.

MXSTEP(n)	*Maximum step-halving allowed.* Specify a positive integer. The default value is 5.
PCONVERGE(a)	*Parameter estimates convergence criterion.* Convergence is assumed if the absolute change or relative change in the parameter estimates is less than this value. The criterion is not used if the value is 0. Specify a nonnegative value. The default value is 10^{-6}.
SINGULAR(a)	*Value used as tolerance in checking singularity.* Specify a positive value. The default value is 10^{-8}.

FULLFACTORIAL Subcommand

The FULLFACTORIAL subcommand generates a specific model: first, the intercept (if included); second, all of the covariates (if specified), in the order in which they are specified; next, all of the main factorial effects; next, all the two-way factorial interaction effects, all of the three-way factorial interaction effects, and so on, up to the highest possible interaction effect.

- The FULLFACTORIAL and the MODEL subcommands are mutually exclusive. Only one of them can be specified at any time.
- The FULLFACTORIAL subcommand does not take any keywords.

INTERCEPT Subcommand

The INTERCEPT subcommand controls whether intercept terms are included in the model. The number of intercept terms is the number of response categories less one.

INCLUDE	*Includes the intercept term.* This is the default.
EXCLUDE	*Excludes the intercept terms.*

MISSING Subcommand

By default, cases with missing values for any of the variables on the NOMREG variable list are excluded from the analysis. The MISSING subcommand allows you to include cases with user-missing values.

- Note that missing values are deleted at the subpopulation level.

EXCLUDE	*Excludes both user-missing and system-missing values.* This is the default.
INCLUDE	*User-missing values are treated as valid.* System-missing values cannot be included in the analysis.

MODEL Subcommand

The MODEL subcommand specifies the effects in the model.

- The MODEL and the FULLFACTORIAL subcommands are mutually exclusive. Only one of them can be specified at any time.

- If more than one MODEL subcommand is specified, only the last one is in effect.

- Specify a list of terms to be included in the model, separated by commas or spaces. If the MODEL subcommand is omitted or empty, the default model is generated. The default model contains: first, the intercept (if included); second, all of the covariates (if specified), in the order in which they are specified; and next, all of the main factorial effects, in the order in which they are specified.

- To include a main-effect term, enter the name of the factor on the MODEL subcommand.

- To include an interaction-effect term among factors, use the keyword BY or the asterisk (*) to join factors involved in the interaction. For example, A*B*C means a three-way interaction effect of A, B, and C, where A, B, and C are factors. The expression A BY B BY C is equivalent to A*B*C. Factors inside an interaction effect must be distinct. Expressions like A*C*A and A*A are invalid.

- To include a nested effect term, use the keyword WITHIN or a pair of parentheses on the MODEL subcommand. For example, A(B) means that A is nested within B, where A and B are factors. The expression A WITHIN B is equivalent to A(B). Factors inside a nested effect must be distinct. Expressions like A(A) and A(B*A) are invalid.

- Multiple level nesting is supported. For example, A(B(C)) means that B is nested within C, and A is nested within B(C). When more than one pair of parentheses is present, each pair of parentheses must be enclosed or nested within another pair of parentheses. Thus, A(B)(C) is not valid.

- Nesting within an interaction effect is valid. For example, A(B*C) means that A is nested within B*C.

- Interactions among nested effects are allowed. The correct syntax is the interaction followed by the common nested effect inside the parentheses. For example, interaction between A and B within levels of C should be specified as A*B(C) instead of A(C)*B(C).

- To include a covariate term in the model, enter the name of the covariate on the MODEL subcommand.

- Covariates can be connected, but not nested, using the keyword BY or the asterisk (*) operator. For example, X*X is the product of X and itself. This is equivalent to a covariate whose values are the square of those of X. However, X(Y) is invalid.

- Factor and covariate effects can be connected in many ways. No effects can be nested within a covariate effect. Suppose A and B are factors, and X and Y are covariates. Examples of valid combination of factor and covariate effects are A*X, A*B*X, X(A), X(A*B), X*A(B), X*Y(A*B), and A*B*X*Y.

PRINT Subcommand

The PRINT subcommand displays optional output. If no PRINT subcommand is specified, default output includes a factor information table.

CELLPROB   *Observed proportion, expected probability, and the residual for each covariate pattern and each response category.*

CLASSTABLE	*Classification table.* The square table of frequencies of observed response categories versus the predicted response categories. Each case is classified into the category with the highest predicted probability.
CORB	*Asymptotic correlation matrix of the parameter estimates.*
COVB	*Asymptotic covariance matrix of the parameter estimates.*
FIT	*Goodness-of-fit statistics.* The change in chi-square statistics with respect to a model with intercept terms only (or to a null model when INTERCEPT=EXCLUDE). The table contains the Pearson chi-square and the likelihood-ratio chi-square statistics. The statistics are computed based on the subpopulation classification specified on the SUBPOP subcommand or the default classification.
HISTORY(n)	*Iteration history.* The table contains log-likelihood function value and parameter estimates at every nth iteration beginning with the 0th iteration (the initial estimates). The default is to print every iteration ($n = 1$). The last iteration is always printed if HISTORY is specified, regardless of the value of n.
LRT	*Likelihood-ratio tests.* The table contains the likelihood-ratio test statistics for the model and model partial effects. If LRT is not specified, just the model test statistic is printed.
PARAMETER	*Parameter estimates.*
SUMMARY	*Model summary.* Cox and Snell's, Nagelkerke's, and McFadden's R^2 statistics.

SCALE Subcommand

The SCALE subcommand specifies the dispersion scaling value. Model estimation is not affected by this scaling value. Only the asymptotic covariance matrix of the parameter estimates is affected.

N	*A positive number corresponding to the amount of overdispersion or underdispersion.* The default scaling value is 1, which corresponds to no overdispersion or underdispersion.
DEVIANCE	*Estimates the scaling value by using the deviance function statistic.*
PEARSON	*Estimates the scaling value by using the Pearson chi-square statistic.*

SUBPOP Subcommand

The SUBPOP subcommand allows you to define the subpopulation classification used in computing the goodness-of-fit statistics.

- A variable list is expected if the SUBPOP subcommand is specified. The variables in the list must be a subset of the combined list of factors and covariates specified on the command line.

- Variables specified or implied on the MODEL subcommand must be a subset of the variables specified or implied on the SUBPOP subcommand.
- If the SUBPOP subcommand is omitted, the default classification is based on all of the factors and the covariates specified.
- Missing values are deleted listwise on the subpopulation level.

TEST Subcommand

The TEST subcommand allows you to customize your hypothesis tests by directly specifying null hypotheses as linear combinations of parameters.

- TEST is offered only through syntax.
- Multiple TEST subcommands are allowed. Each is handled independently.
- The basic format for the TEST subcommand is an optional list of values enclosed in parentheses, an optional label in quotes, an effect name or the keyword ALL, and a list of values.
- The value list preceding the first effect or the keyword ALL are the constants to which the linear combinations are equated under the null hypotheses. If this value list is omitted, the constants are assumed to be all zeros.
- The label is a string with a maximum length of 255 characters (or 127 double-byte characters). Only one label per linear combination can be specified.
- When ALL is specified, only a list of values can follow. The number of values must equal the number of parameters (including the redundant ones) in the model.
- When effects are specified, only valid effects appearing or implied on the MODEL subcommand can be named. The number of values following an effect name must equal the number of parameters (including the redundant ones) corresponding to that effect. For example, if the effect A*B takes up six parameters, then exactly six values must follow A*B. To specify the coefficient for the intercept, use the keyword INTERCEPT. Only one value is expected to follow INTERCEPT.
- When multiple linear combinations are specified within the same TEST subcommand, use semicolons to separate each hypothesis.
- The linear combinations are first separately tested for each logit, and then simultaneously tested for all of the logits.
- A number can be specified as a fraction with a positive denominator. For example, 1/3 or –1/3 are valid, but 1/–3 is invalid.
- Effects appearing or implied on the MODEL subcommand but not specified on the TEST are assumed to take the value 0 for all of their parameters.

NLR

```
MODEL PROGRAM parameter=value [parameter=value ...]
transformation commands

[DERIVATIVES
transformation commands]

[CLEAR MODEL PROGRAMS]
```

Procedure CNLR (Constrained Nonlinear Regression):

```
[CONSTRAINED FUNCTIONS
transformation commands]

CNLR dependent var

 [/FILE=file]   [/OUTFILE=file]

 [/PRED=varname]

 [/SAVE [PRED] [RESID[(varname)]] [DERIVATIVES] [LOSS]]

 [/CRITERIA=[ITER n] [MITER n] [CKDER {0.5**}]
                                     {n    }
             [ISTEP {1E+20**}] [FPR n] [LFTOL n]
                    {n      }
             [LSTOL n] [STEPLIMIT {2**}] [NFTOL n]
                                  {n  }
             [FTOL n] [OPTOL n] [CRSHTOL {.01**}]]]
                                         {n    }

 [/BOUNDS=expression, expression, ...]

 [/LOSS=varname]

 [/BOOTSTRAP [=n]]
```

Procedure NLR (Nonlinear Regression):

```
NLR dependent var

 [/FILE=file]   [/OUTFILE=file]

 [/PRED=varname]

 [/SAVE [PRED] [RESID [(varname)] [DERIVATIVES]]

 [/CRITERIA=[ITER {100**}] [CKDER {0.5**}]
                  {n    }         {n    }
             [SSCON {1E-8**}]  [PCON {1E-8**}]   [RCON {1E-8**}]]
                    {n     }         {n     }          {n     }
```

**Default if the subcommand or keyword is omitted.

Example:

```
MODEL PROGRAM A=.6.
COMPUTE PRED=EXP(A*X).

NLR Y.
```

Overview

Nonlinear regression is used to estimate parameter values and regression statistics for models that are not linear in their parameters. SPSS has two procedures for estimating nonlinear equations. CNLR (constrained nonlinear regression), which uses a sequential quadratic programming algorithm, is applicable for both constrained and unconstrained problems. NLR (nonlinear regression), which uses a Levenberg-Marquardt algorithm, is applicable only for unconstrained problems.

CNLR is more general. It allows linear and nonlinear constraints on any combination of parameters. It will estimate parameters by minimizing any smooth loss function (objective function), and can optionally compute bootstrap estimates of parameter standard errors and correlations. The individual bootstrap parameter estimates can optionally be saved in a separate SPSS data file.

Both programs estimate the values of the parameters for the model and, optionally, compute and save predicted values, residuals, and derivatives. Final parameter estimates can be saved in an SPSS data file and used in subsequent analyses.

CNLR and NLR use much of the same syntax. Some of the following sections discuss features common to both procedures. In these sections, the notation [C]NLR means that either the CNLR or NLR procedure can be specified. Sections that apply only to CNLR or only to NLR are clearly identified.

Options

The Model. You can use any number of transformation commands under MODEL PROGRAM to define complex models.

Derivatives. You can use any number of transformation commands under DERIVATIVES to supply derivatives.

Adding Variables to Working Data File. You can add predicted values, residuals, and derivatives to the working data file with the SAVE subcommand.

Writing Parameter Estimates to a New Data File. You can save final parameter estimates as an external SPSS data file using the OUTFILE subcommand; you can retrieve them in subsequent analyses using the FILE subcommand.

Controlling Model-Building Criteria. You can control the iteration process used in the regression with the CRITERIA subcommand.

Additional CNLR Controls. For CNLR, you can impose linear and nonlinear constraints on the parameters with the BOUNDS subcommand. Using the LOSS subcommand, you can specify a loss function for CNLR to minimize and, using the BOOTSTRAP subcommand, you can provide bootstrap estimates of the parameter standard errors, confidence intervals, and correlations.

Basic Specification

The basic specification requires three commands: MODEL PROGRAM, COMPUTE (or any other computational transformation command), and [C]NLR.

- The MODEL PROGRAM command assigns initial values to the parameters and signifies the beginning of the model program.
- The computational transformation command generates a new variable to define the model. The variable can take any legitimate name, but if the name is not *PRED*, the PRED subcommand will be required.
- The [C]NLR command provides the regression specifications. The minimum specification is the dependent variable.
- By default, the residual sum of squares and estimated values of the model parameters are displayed for each iteration. Statistics generated include regression and residual sums of squares and mean squares, corrected and uncorrected total sums of squares, R^2, parameter estimates with their asymptotic standard errors and 95% confidence intervals, and an asymptotic correlation matrix of the parameter estimates.

Command Order

- The model program, beginning with the MODEL PROGRAM command, must precede the [C]NLR command.
- The derivatives program (when used), beginning with the DERIVATIVES command, must follow the model program but precede the [C]NLR command.
- The constrained functions program (when used), beginning with the CONSTRAINED FUNCTIONS command, must immediately precede the CNLR command. The constrained functions program cannot be used with the NLR command.
- The CNLR command must follow the block of transformations for the model program and the derivatives program when specified; the CNLR command must also follow the constrained functions program when specified.
- Subcommands on [C]NLR can be named in any order.

Syntax Rules

- The FILE, OUTFILE, PRED, and SAVE subcommands work the same way for both CNLR and NLR.
- The CRITERIA subcommand is used by both CNLR and NLR, but iteration criteria are different. Therefore, the CRITERIA subcommand is documented separately for CNLR and NLR.
- The BOUNDS, LOSS, and BOOTSTRAP subcommands can be used only with CNLR. They cannot be used with NLR.

Operations

- By default, the predicted values, residuals, and derivatives are created as temporary variables. To save these variables, use the SAVE subcommand.

Weighting Cases

- If case weighting is in effect, [C]NLR uses case weights when calculating the residual sum of squares and derivatives. However, the degrees of freedom in the ANOVA table are always based on unweighted cases.

- When the model program is first invoked for each case, the weight variable's value is set equal to its value in the working data file. The model program may recalculate that value. For example, to effect a robust estimation, the model program may recalculate the weight variable's value as an inverse function of the residual magnitude. [C]NLR uses the weight variable's value after the model program is executed.

Missing Values

Cases with missing values for any of the dependent or independent variables named on the [C]NLR command are excluded.

- Predicted values, but not residuals, can be calculated for cases with missing values on the dependent variable.

- [C]NLR ignores cases that have missing, negative, or zero weights. The procedure displays a warning message if it encounters any negative or zero weights at any time during its execution.

- If a variable used in the model program or the derivatives program is omitted from the independent variable list on the [C]NLR command, the predicted value and some or all of the derivatives may be missing for every case. If this happens, SPSS generates an error message.

Example

```
MODEL PROGRAM A=.5 B=1.6.
COMPUTE PRED=A*SPEED**B.

DERIVATIVES.
COMPUTE D.A=SPEED**B.
COMPUTE D.B=A*LN(SPEED)*SPEED**B.

NLR STOP.
```

- MODEL PROGRAM assigns values to the model parameters *A* and *B*.

- COMPUTE generates the variable *PRED* to define the nonlinear model using parameters *A* and *B* and the variable *SPEED* from the working data file. Because this variable is named *PRED*, the PRED subcommand is not required on NLR.

- DERIVATIVES indicates that calculations for derivatives are being supplied.

- The two COMPUTE statements on the DERIVATIVES transformations list calculate the derivatives for the parameters *A* and *B*. If either one had been omitted, NLR would have calculated it numerically.

- NLR specifies *STOP* as the dependent variable. It is not necessary to specify *SPEED* as the independent variable since it has been used in the model and derivatives programs.

MODEL PROGRAM Command

The MODEL PROGRAM command assigns initial values to the parameters and signifies the beginning of the model program. The model program specifies the nonlinear equation chosen to model the data. There is no default model.

- The model program is required and must precede the [C]NLR command.
- The MODEL PROGRAM command must specify all parameters in the model program. Each parameter must be individually named. Keyword TO is not allowed.
- Parameters can be assigned any acceptable SPSS variable name. However, if you intend to write the final parameter estimates to a file with the OUTFILE subcommand, do not use the name *SSE* or *NCASES* (see the OUTFILE subcommand on p. 151).
- Each parameter in the model program must have an assigned value. The value can be specified on MODEL PROGRAM or read from an existing parameter data file named on the FILE subcommand.
- Zero should be avoided as an initial value because it provides no information on the scale of the parameters. This is especially true for CNLR.
- The model program must include at least one command that uses the parameters and the independent variables (or preceding transformations of these) to calculate the predicted value of the dependent variable. This predicted value defines the nonlinear model. There is no default model.
- By default, the program assumes that *PRED* is the name assigned to the variable for the predicted values. If you use a different variable name in the model program, you must supply the name on the PRED subcommand (see the PRED subcommand on p. 152).
- In the model program, you can assign a label to the variable holding predicted values and also change its print and write formats, but you should not specify missing values for this variable.
- You can use any computational commands (such as COMPUTE, IF, DO IF, LOOP, END LOOP, END IF, RECODE, or COUNT) or output commands (WRITE, PRINT, or XSAVE) in the model program, but you cannot use input commands (such as DATA LIST, GET, MATCH FILES, or ADD FILES).
- Transformations in the model program are used only by [C]NLR, and they do not affect the working data file. The parameters created by the model program do not become a part of the working data file. Permanent transformations should be specified before the model program.

Caution

The selection of good initial values for the parameters in the model program is very important to the operation of [C]NLR. The selection of poor initial values can result in no solution, a local rather than a general solution, or a physically impossible solution.

Example

```
MODEL PROGRAM A=10 B=1 C=5 D=1.
COMPUTE PRED= A*exp(B*X) + C*exp(D*X).
```

- The MODEL PROGRAM command assigns starting values to the four parameters *A*, *B*, *C*, and *D*.
- COMPUTE defines the model to be fit as the sum of two exponentials.

DERIVATIVES Command

The optional DERIVATIVES command signifies the beginning of the derivatives program. The derivatives program contains transformation statements for computing some or all of the derivatives of the model. The derivatives program must follow the model program but precede the [C]NLR command.

If the derivatives program is not used, [C]NLR numerically estimates derivatives for all the parameters. Providing derivatives reduces computation time and, in some situations, may result in a better solution.

- The DERIVATIVES command has no further specifications but must be followed by the set of transformation statements that calculate the derivatives.
- You can use any computational commands (such as COMPUTE, IF, DO IF, LOOP, END LOOP, END IF, RECODE, or COUNT) or output commands (WRITE, PRINT, or XSAVE) in the derivatives program, but you cannot use input commands (such as DATA LIST, GET, MATCH FILES, or ADD FILES).
- To name the derivatives, specify the prefix *D.* before each parameter name. For example, the derivative name for the parameter *PARM1* must be *D.PARM1*.
- Once a derivative has been calculated by a transformation, the variable for that derivative can be used in subsequent transformations.
- You do not need to supply all of the derivatives. Those that are not supplied will be estimated by the program. During the first iteration of the nonlinear estimation procedure, derivatives calculated in the derivatives program are compared with numerically calculated derivatives. This serves as a check on the supplied values (see the CRITERIA subcommand on p. 154).
- Transformations in the derivatives program are used by [C]NLR only and do not affect the working data file.
- For NLR, the derivative of each parameter must be computed with respect to the predicted function. (For computation of derivatives in CNLR, see the LOSS subcommand on p. 158.)

Example

```
MODEL PROGRAM A=1, B=0, C=1, D=0
COMPUTE PRED = Ae^Bx + Ce^Dx
DERIVATIVES.
COMPUTE D.A = exp (B * X).
COMPUTE D.B = A * exp (B * X) * X.
COMPUTE D.C = exp (D * X).
COMPUTE D.D = C * exp (D * X) * X.
```

- The derivatives program specifies derivatives of the PRED function for the sum of the two exponentials in the model described by the following equation:

$$Y = Ae^{Bx} + Ce^{Dx}$$

Example

```
DERIVATIVES.
COMPUTE D.A = exp (B * X).
COMPUTE D.B = A * X * D.A.
COMPUTE D.C = exp (D * X).
COMPUTE D.D = C * X * D.C.
```

- This is an alternative way to express the same derivatives program specified in the previous example.

CONSTRAINED FUNCTIONS Command

The optional CONSTRAINED FUNCTIONS command signifies the beginning of the constrained functions program, which specifies nonlinear constraints. The constrained functions program is specified after the model program and the derivatives program (when used). It can only be used with, and must precede, the CNLR command. For more information, see the BOUNDS subcommand on p. 157.

Example

```
MODEL PROGRAM A=.5 B=1.6.
COMPUTE PRED=A*SPEED**B.

CONSTRAINED FUNCTIONS.
COMPUTE CF=A-EXP(B).

CNLR STOP
  /BOUNDS CF LE 0.
```

CLEAR MODEL PROGRAMS Command

CLEAR MODEL PROGRAMS deletes all transformations associated with the model program, the derivative program, and/or the constrained functions program previously submitted. It is primarily used in interactive mode to remove temporary variables created by these programs without affecting the working data file or variables created by other transformation programs or temporary programs. It allows you to specify new models, derivatives, or constrained functions without having to run [C]NLR.

It is not necessary to use this command if you have already executed the [C]NLR procedure. Temporary variables associated with the procedure are automatically deleted.

CNLR/NLR Command

Either the CNLR or the NLR command is required to specify the dependent and independent variables for the nonlinear regression.

- For either CNLR or NLR, the minimum specification is a dependent variable.
- Only one dependent variable can be specified. It must be a numeric variable in the working data file and cannot be a variable generated by the model or the derivatives program.

OUTFILE Subcommand

OUTFILE stores final parameter estimates for use on a subsequent [C]NLR command. The only specification on OUTFILE is the target file. Some or all of the values from this file can be read into a subsequent [C]NLR procedure with the FILE subcommand. The parameter data file created by OUTFILE stores the following variables:

- All of the split-file variables. OUTFILE writes one case of values for each split-file group in the working data file.
- All of the parameters named on the MODEL PROGRAM command.
- The labels, formats, and missing values of the split-file variables and parameters defined for them previous to their use in the [C]NLR procedure.
- The sum of squared residuals (named *SSE*). *SSE* has no labels or missing values. The print and write format for *SSE* is F10.8.
- The number of cases on which the analysis was based (named *NCASES*). *NCASES* has no labels or missing values. The print and write format for *NCASES* is F8.0.

When OUTFILE is used, the model program cannot create variables named *SSE* or *NCASES*.

Example

```
MODEL PROGRAM A=.5 B=1.6.
COMPUTE PRED=A*SPEED**B.
NLR STOP /OUTFILE=PARAM.
```

- OUTFILE generates a parameter data file containing one case for four variables: *A*, *B*, *SSE*, and *NCASES*.

FILE Subcommand

FILE reads starting values for the parameters from a parameter data file created by an OUTFILE subcommand from a previous [C]NLR procedure. When starting values are read from a file, they do not have to be specified on the MODEL PROGRAM command. Rather, the MODEL PROGRAM command simply names the parameters that correspond to the parameters in the data file.

- The only specification on FILE is the file that contains the starting values.
- Some new parameters may be specified for the model on the MODEL PROGRAM command while others are read from the file specified on the FILE subcommand.
- You do not have to name the parameters on MODEL PROGRAM in the order in which they occur in the parameter data file. In addition, you can name a partial list of the variables contained in the file.
- If the starting value for a parameter is specified on MODEL PROGRAM, the specification overrides the value read from the parameter data file.
- If split-file processing is in effect, the starting values for the first subfile are taken from the first case of the parameter data file. Subfiles are matched with cases in order until the starting value file runs out of cases. All subsequent subfiles use the starting values for the last case.

- To read starting values from a parameter data file and then replace those values with the final results from [C]NLR, specify the same file on the FILE and OUTFILE subcommands. The input file is read completely before anything is written in the output file.

Example

```
MODEL PROGRAM A B C=1 D=3.
COMPUTE PRED=A*SPEED**B + C*SPEED**D.
NLR STOP /FILE=PARAM /OUTFILE=PARAM.
```

- MODEL PROGRAM names four of the parameters used to calculate *PRED*, but assigns values to only *C* and *D*. The values of *A* and *B* are read from the existing data file *PARAM*.
- After NLR computes the final estimates of the four parameters, OUTFILE writes over the old input file. If, in addition to these new final estimates, the former starting values of *A* and *B* are still desired, specify a different file on the OUTFILE subcommand.

PRED Subcommand

PRED identifies the variable holding the predicted values.

- The only specification is a variable name, which must be identical to the variable name used to calculate predicted values in the model program.
- If the model program names the variable *PRED*, the PRED subcommand can be omitted. Otherwise, the PRED subcommand is required.
- The variable for predicted values is not saved in the working data file unless the SAVE subcommand is used.

Example

```
MODEL PROGRAM A=.5 B=1.6.
COMPUTE PSTOP=A*SPEED**B.
NLR STOP /PRED=PSTOP.
```

- COMPUTE in the model program creates a variable named *PSTOP* to temporarily store the predicted values for the dependent variable *STOP*.
- PRED identifies *PSTOP* as the variable used to define the model for the NLR procedure.

SAVE Subcommand

SAVE is used to save the temporary variables for the predicted values, residuals, and derivatives created by the model and the derivatives programs.

- The minimum specification is a single keyword.
- The variables to be saved must have unique names on the working data file. If a naming conflict exists, the variables are not saved.
- Temporary variables, for example, variables created after a TEMPORARY command and parameters specified by the model program, are not saved in the working data file. They will not cause naming conflicts.

The following keywords are available and can be used in any combination and in any order. The new variables are always appended to the working data file in the order in which these keywords are presented here:

PRED   *Save the predicted values.* The variable's name, label, and formats are those specified for it (or assigned by default) in the model program.

RESID [(varname)] *Save the residuals variable.* You can specify a variable name in parentheses following the keyword. If no variable name is specified, the name of this variable is the same as the specification you use for this keyword. For example, if you use the three-character abbreviation RES, the default variable name will be *RES*. The variable has the same print and write format as the predicted values variable created by the model program. It has no variable label and no user-defined missing values. It is system-missing for any case in which either the dependent variable is missing or the predicted value cannot be computed.

DERIVATIVES   *Save the derivative variables.* The derivative variables are named with the prefix *D.* to the first six characters of the parameter names. Derivative variables use the print and write formats of the predicted values variable and have no value labels or user-missing values. Derivative variables are saved in the same order as the parameters named on MODEL PROGRAM. Derivatives are saved for all parameters, whether or not the derivative was supplied in the derivatives program.

LOSS   *Save the user-specified loss function variable.* This specification is available only with CNLR and only if the LOSS subcommand has been specified.

Asymptotic standard errors of predicted values and residuals, and special residuals used for outlier detection and influential case analysis are not provided by the [C]NLR procedure. However, for a squared loss function, the asymptotically correct values for all these statistics can be calculated using the SAVE subcommand with [C]NLR and then using the REGRESSION procedure. In REGRESSION, the dependent variable is still the same, and derivatives of the model parameters are used as independent variables. Casewise plots, standard errors of prediction, partial regression plots, and other diagnostics of the regression are valid for the non-linear model.

Example

```
MODEL PROGRAM A=.5 B=1.6.
COMPUTE PSTOP=A*SPEED**B.
NLR STOP /PRED=PSTOP
  /SAVE=RESID(RSTOP) DERIVATIVES PRED.
REGRESSION VARIABLES=STOP D.A D.B /ORIGIN
  /DEPENDENT=STOP /ENTER D.A D.B /RESIDUALS.
```

- The SAVE subcommand creates the residuals variable *RSTOP* and the derivative variables *D.A* and *D.B*.

- Because the PRED subcommand identifies *PSTOP* as the variable for predicted values in the nonlinear model, keyword PRED on SAVE adds the variable *PSTOP* to the working data file.

- The new variables are added to the working data file in the following order: *PSTOP,
  RSTOP, D.A,* and *D.B.*
- The subcommand RESIDUALS for REGRESSION produces the default analysis of residuals.

CRITERIA Subcommand

CRITERIA controls the values of the cutoff points used to stop the iterative calculations in [C]NLR.

- The minimum specification is any of the criteria keywords and an appropriate value. The value can be specified in parentheses after an equals sign, a space, or a comma. Multiple keywords can be specified in any order. Defaults are in effect for keywords not specified.
- Keywords available for CRITERIA differ between CNLR and NLR and are discussed separately. However, with both CNLR and NLR, you can specify the critical value for derivative checking.

Checking Derivatives for CNLR and NLR

Upon entering the first iteration, [C]NLR always checks any derivatives calculated on the derivatives program by comparing them with numerically calculated derivatives. For each comparison, it computes an agreement score. A score of 1 indicates agreement to machine precision; a score of 0 indicates definite disagreement. If a score is less than 1, either an incorrect derivative was supplied or there were numerical problems in estimating the derivative. The lower the score, the more likely it is that the supplied derivatives are incorrect. Highly correlated parameters may cause disagreement even when a correct derivative is supplied. Be sure to check the derivatives if the agreement score is not 1.

During the first iteration, [C]NLR checks each derivative score. If any score is below 1, it begins displaying a table to show the worst (lowest) score for each derivative. If any score is below the critical value, the program stops.

To specify the critical value, use the following keyword on CRITERIA:

CKDER n   *Critical value for derivative checking.* Specify a number between 0 and 1 for *n*. The default is 0.5. Specify 0 to disable this criterion.

Iteration Criteria for CNLR

The CNLR procedure uses NPSOL (Version 4.0) Fortran Package for Nonlinear Programming (Gill et al., 1986). The CRITERIA subcommand of CNLR gives the control features of NPSOL. The following section summarizes the NPSOL documentation.

CNLR uses a sequential quadratic programming algorithm, with a quadratic programming subproblem to determine the search direction. If constraints or bounds are specified, the first step is to find a point that is feasible with respect to those constraints. Each major iteration sets up a quadratic program to find the search direction, *p*. Minor iterations are used to solve this subproblem. Then, the major iteration determines a steplength α by a line search, and the function is evaluated at the new point. An optimal solution is found when the optimality tolerance criterion is met.

The CRITERIA subcommand has the following keywords when used with CNLR:

ITER n

Maximum number of major iterations. Specify any positive integer for *n*. The default is $\max(50, 3(p + m_L) + 10m_N)$, where p is the number of parameters, m_L is the number of linear constraints, and m_N is the number of nonlinear constraints. If the search for a solution stops because this limit is exceeded, CNLR issues a warning message.

MINORITERATION n

Maximum number of minor iterations. Specify any positive integer. This is the number of minor iterations allowed within each major iteration. The default is $\max(50, 3(n + m_L + m_N))$.

CRSHTOL n

Crash tolerance. CRSHTOL is used to determine if initial values are within their specified bounds. Specify any value between 0 and 1. The default value is 0.01. A constraint of the form $a'X \geq l$ is considered a valid part of the working set if $|a'X - l| < \text{CRSHTOL}(1 + |l|)$.

STEPLIMIT n

Step limit. The CNLR algorithm does not allow changes in the length of the parameter vector to exceed a factor of *n*. The limit prevents very early steps from going too far from good initial estimates. Specify any positive value. The default value is 2.

FTOLERANCE n

Feasibility tolerance. This is the maximum absolute difference allowed for both linear and nonlinear constraints for a solution to be considered feasible. Specify any value greater than 0. The default value is the square root of your machine's epsilon.

LFTOLERANCE n

Linear feasibility tolerance. If specified, this overrides FTOLERANCE for linear constraints and bounds. Specify any value greater than 0. The default value is the square root of your machine's epsilon.

NFTOLERANCE n

Nonlinear feasibility tolerance. If specified, this overrides FTOLERANCE for nonlinear constraints. Specify any value greater than 0. The default value is the square root of your machine's epsilon.

LSTOLERANCE n

Line search tolerance. This value must be between 0 and 1 (but not including 1). It controls the accuracy required of the line search that forms the innermost search loop. The default value, 0.9, specifies an inaccurate search. This is appropriate for many problems, particularly if nonlinear constraints are involved. A smaller positive value, corresponding to a more accurate line search, may give better performance if there are no nonlinear constraints, all (or most) derivatives are supplied in the derivatives program, and the data fit in memory.

OPTOLERANCE n

Optimality tolerance. If an iteration point is a feasible point and the next step will not produce a relative change in either the parameter vector or the objective function of more than the square root of OPTOLERANCE, an optimal solution has been found. OPTOLERANCE can also be thought of as the number of significant digits in the objective function at the solution. For example, if OPTOLERANCE=10^{-6}, the objective function should have approximately six significant digits of accuracy. Specify any number between the FPRECISION value and 1. The default value for OPTOLERANCE is epsilon**0.8.

FPRECISION n   *Function precision.* This is a measure of the accuracy with which the objective function can be checked. It acts as a relative precision when the function is large, and an absolute precision when the function is small. For example, if the objective function is larger than 1, and six significant digits are desired, FPRECISION should be $1E-6$. If, however, the objective function is of the order 0.001, FPRECISION should be $1E-9$ to get six digits of accuracy. Specify any number between 0 and 1. The choice of FPRECISION can be very complicated for a badly scaled problem. Chapter 8 of Gill et al. (1981) gives some scaling suggestions. The default value is epsilon**0.9.

ISTEP n   *Infinite step size.* This value is the magnitude of the change in parameters that is defined as infinite. That is, if the change in the parameters at a step is greater than ISTEP, the problem is considered unbounded, and estimation stops. Specify any positive number. The default value is $1E+20$.

Iteration Criteria for NLR

The NLR procedure uses an adaptation of subroutine LMSTR from the MINPACK package by Garbow et al. Because the NLR algorithm differs substantially from CNLR, the CRITERIA subcommand for NLR has a different set of keywords.

NLR computes parameter estimates using the Levenberg-Marquardt method. At each iteration, NLR evaluates the estimates against a set of control criteria. The iterative calculations continue until one of five cutoff points is met, at which point the iterations stop and the reason for stopping is displayed.

The CRITERIA subcommand has the following keywords when used with NLR:

ITER n   *Maximum number of major and minor iterations allowed.* Specify any positive integer for *n*. The default is 100 iterations per parameter. If the search for a solution stops because this limit is exceeded, NLR issues a warning message.

SSCON n   *Convergence criterion for the sum of squares.* Specify any non-negative number for *n*. The default is $1E-8$. If successive iterations fail to reduce the sum of squares by this proportion, the procedure stops. Specify 0 to disable this criterion.

PCON n   *Convergence criterion for the parameter values.* Specify any non-negative number for *n*. The default is $1E-8$. If successive iterations fail to change any of the parameter values by this proportion, the procedure stops. Specify 0 to disable this criterion.

RCON n   *Convergence criterion for the correlation between the residuals and the derivatives.* Specify any non-negative number for *n*. The default is $1E-8$. If the largest value for the correlation between the residuals and the derivatives equals this value, the procedure stops because it lacks the information it needs to estimate a direction for its next move. This criterion is often referred to as a gradient convergence criterion. Specify 0 to disable this criterion.

Example

```
MODEL PROGRAM A=.5 B=1.6.
COMPUTE PRED=A*SPEED**B.
NLR STOP /CRITERIA=ITER(80) SSCON=.000001.
```

- CRITERIA changes two of the five cutoff values affecting iteration, ITER and SSCON, and leaves the remaining three, PCON, RCON, and CKDER, at their default values.

BOUNDS Subcommand

The BOUNDS subcommand can be used to specify both linear and nonlinear constraints. It can be used only with CNLR; it cannot be used with NLR.

Simple Bounds and Linear Constraints

BOUNDS can be used to impose bounds on parameter values. These bounds can involve either single parameters or a linear combination of parameters and can be either equalities or inequalities.

- All bounds are specified on the same BOUNDS subcommand and separated by semicolons.
- The only variables allowed on BOUNDS are parameter variables (those named on MODEL PROGRAM).
- Only * (multiplication), + (addition), – (subtraction), = or EQ, >= or GE, and <= or LE can be used. When two relational operators are used (as in the third bound in the example below), they must both be in the same direction.

Example

```
/BOUNDS 5 >= A;
        B >= 9;
        .01 <= 2*A + C <= 1;
        D + 2*E = 10
```

- BOUNDS imposes bounds on the parameters *A*, *B*, *C*, and *D*. Specifications for each parameter are separated by a semicolon.

Nonlinear Constraints

Nonlinear constraints on the parameters can also be specified with the BOUNDS subcommand. The constrained function must be calculated and stored in a variable by a constrained functions program directly preceding the CNLR command. The constraint is then specified on the BOUNDS subcommand.

In general, nonlinear bounds will not be obeyed until an optimal solution has been found. This is different from simple and linear bounds, which are satisfied at each iteration. The constrained functions must be smooth near the solution.

Example

```
MODEL PROGRAM A=.5 B=1.6.
COMPUTE PRED=A*SPEED**B.

CONSTRAINED FUNCTIONS.
COMPUTE DIFF=A-10**B.

CNLR STOP /BOUNDS DIFF LE 0.
```

- The constrained function is calculated by a constrained functions program and stored in variable *DIFF*. The constrained functions program immediately precedes CNLR.
- BOUNDS imposes bounds on the function (less than or equal to 0).
- CONSTRAINED FUNCTIONS variables and parameters named on MODEL PROGRAM cannot be combined in the same BOUNDS expression. For example, you *cannot* specify $(DIFF + A) > = 0$ on the BOUNDS subcommand.

LOSS Subcommand

LOSS specifies a loss function for CNLR to minimize. By default, CNLR minimizes the sum of squared residuals. LOSS can be used only with CNLR; it cannot be used with NLR.

- The loss function must first be computed in the model program. LOSS is then used to specify the name of the computed variable.
- The minimizing algorithm may fail if it is given a loss function that is not smooth, such as the absolute value of residuals.
- If derivatives are supplied, the derivative of each parameter must be computed with respect to the loss function, rather than the predicted value. The easiest way to do this is in two steps: first compute derivatives of the model, and then compute derivatives of the loss function with respect to the model and multiply by the model derivatives.
- When LOSS is used, the usual summary statistics are not computed. Standard errors, confidence intervals, and correlations of the parameters are available only if the BOOTSTRAP subcommand is specified.

Example

```
MODEL PROGRAM  A=1 B=1.
COMPUTE PRED=EXP(A+B*T)/(1+EXP(A+B*T)).
COMPUTE LOSS=-W*(Y*LN(PRED)+(1-Y)*LN(1-PRED)).

DERIVATIVES.
COMPUTE D.A=PRED/(1+EXP(A+B*T)).
COMPUTE D.B=T*PRED/(1+EXP(A+B*T)).
COMPUTE D.A=(-W*(Y/PRED - (1-Y)/(1-PRED)) * D.A).
COMPUTE D.B=(-W*(Y/PRED - (1-Y)/(1-PRED)) * D.B).

CNLR Y /LOSS=LOSS.
```

- The second COMPUTE command in the model program computes the loss functions and stores its values in the variable *LOSS*, which is then specified on the LOSS subcommand.
- Because derivatives are supplied in the derivatives program, the derivatives of all parameters are computed with respect to the loss function, rather than the predicted value.

BOOTSTRAP Subcommand

BOOTSTRAP provides bootstrap estimates of the parameter standard errors, confidence intervals, and correlations. BOOTSTRAP can be used only with CNLR; it cannot be used with NLR.

Bootstrapping is a way of estimating the standard error of a statistic, using repeated samples from the original data set. This is done by sampling with replacement to get samples of the same size as the original data set.

- The minimum specification is the subcommand keyword. Optionally, specify the number of samples to use for generating bootstrap results.

- By default, BOOTSTRAP generates bootstrap results based on $10*p*(p+1)/2$ samples, where p is the number of parameters. That is, 10 samples are drawn for each statistic (standard error or correlation) to be calculated.

- When BOOTSTRAP is used, the nonlinear equation is estimated for each sample. The standard error of each parameter estimate is then calculated as the standard deviation of the bootstrapped estimates. Parameter values from the original data are used as starting values for each bootstrap sample. Even so, bootstrapping is computationally expensive.

- If the OUTFILE subcommand is specified, a case is written to the output file for each bootstrap sample. The first case in the file will be the actual parameter estimates, followed by the bootstrap samples. After the first case is eliminated (using SELECT IF), other SPSS procedures (such as FREQUENCIES) can be used to examine the bootstrap distribution.

Example

```
MODEL PROGRAM A=.5 B=1.6.
COMPUTE PSTOP=A*SPEED**B.
CNLR STOP /BOOTSTRAP /OUTFILE=PARAM.
GET FILE=PARAM.
LIST.
COMPUTE ID=$CASENUM.
SELECT IF (ID > 1).
FREQUENCIES A B /FORMAT=NOTABLE /HISTOGRAM.
```

- CNLR generates the bootstrap standard errors, confidence intervals, and parameter correlation matrix. OUTFILE saves the bootstrap estimates in the file *PARAM*.

- GET retrieves the system file *PARAM*.

- LIST lists the different sample estimates along with the original estimate. *NCASES* in the listing (see the OUTFILE subcommand on p. 151) refers to the number of distinct cases in the sample because cases are duplicated in each bootstrap sample.

- FREQUENCIES generates histograms of the bootstrapped parameter estimates.

PROBIT

```
PROBIT response-count varname OF observation-count varname
       WITH varlist [BY varname(min,max)]

[/MODEL={PROBIT**}]
       {LOGIT    }
       {BOTH     }

[/LOG=[{10**  }]
       {2.718}
       {value}
       {NONE  }

[/CRITERIA=[{OPTOL    }({epsilon**0.8})]][P({0.15**})][STEPLIMIT({0.1**})]
            {CONVERGE} {n           }    {p       }             {n      }

            [ITERATE({max(50,3(p+1)**})]]
                     {n              }

[/NATRES[=value]]

[/PRINT={{CI**] [FREQ**] [RMP**]} [PARALL] [NONE] [ALL]]
        {DEFAULT**                }

[/MISSING=[{EXCLUDE**}]   ]
           {INCLUDE   }
```

**Default if the subcommand or keyword is omitted.

Example:

```
PROBIT  R OF N BY ROOT(1,2) WITH X
   /MODEL = BOTH.
```

Overview

PROBIT can be used to estimate the effects of one or more independent variables on a dichotomous dependent variable (such as dead or alive, employed or unemployed, product purchased or not). The program is designed for dose-response analyses and related models, but PROBIT can also estimate logistic regression models.

Options

The Model. You can request a probit or logit response model, or both, for the observed response proportions with the MODEL subcommand.

Transform Predictors. You can control the base of the log transformation applied to the predictors or request no log transformation with the LOG subcommand.

Natural Response Rates. You can instruct PROBIT to estimate the natural response rate (threshold) of the model or supply a known natural response rate to be used in the solution with the NATRES subcommand.

Algorithm Control Parameters. You can specify values of algorithm control parameters, such as the limit on iterations, using the CRITERIA subcommand.

Statistics. By default, PROBIT calculates frequencies, fiducial confidence intervals, and the relative median potency. It also produces a plot of the observed probits or logits against the values of a single independent variable. Optionally, you can use the PRINT subcommand to request a test of the parallelism of regression lines for different levels of the grouping variable or to suppress any or all of these statistics.

Basic Specification

- The basic specification is the response-count variable, keyword OF, the observation-count variable, keyword WITH, and at least one independent variable.
- PROBIT calculates maximum-likelihood estimates for the parameters of the default probit response model and automatically displays estimates of the regression coefficient and intercept terms, their standard errors, a covariance matrix of parameter estimates, and a Pearson chi-square goodness-of-fit test of the model.

Subcommand Order

- The variable specification must be first.
- Subcommands can be named in any order.

Syntax Rules

- The variables must include a response count, an observation count, and at least one predictor. A categorical grouping variable is optional.
- All subcommands are optional and each can appear only once.
- Generally, data should not be entered for individual observations. PROBIT expects predictor values, response counts, and the total number of observations as the input case.
- If the data are available only in a case-by-case form, use AGGREGATE first to compute the required response and observation counts.

Operations

- The transformed response variable is predicted as a linear function of other variables using the nonlinear-optimization method. Note that the previous releases used the iteratively weighted least-squares method, which has a different way of transforming the response variables. See the MODEL subcommand on p. 164.
- If individual cases are entered in the data, PROBIT skips the plot of transformed response proportions and predictor values.
- If individual cases are entered, the degrees of freedom for the chi-square goodness-of-fit statistic are based on the individual cases.

Limitations

- Only one prediction model can be tested on a single PROBIT command, although both probit and logit response models can be requested for that prediction.
- Confidence limits, the plot of transformed response proportions and predictor values, and computation of relative median potency are necessarily limited to single-predictor models.

Example

```
PROBIT  R OF N BY ROOT(1,2) WITH X
  /MODEL = BOTH.
```

- This example specifies that both the probit and logit response models be applied to the response frequency *R*, given *N* total observations and the predictor *X*.
- By default, the predictor is log transformed.

Example

```
* Using data in a case-by-case form

DATA LIST FREE / PREPARTN DOSE RESPONSE.
BEGIN DATA
1 1.5 0
  ...
4 20.0 1
END DATA.
COMPUTE SUBJECT = 1.
PROBIT RESPONSE OF SUBJECT BY PREPARTN(1,4) WITH DOSE.
```

- This dose-response model (Finney, 1971) illustrates a case-by-case analysis. A researcher tests four different preparations at varying doses and observes whether each subject responds. The data are individually recorded for each subject, with 1 indicating a response and 0 indicating no response. The number of observations is always 1 and is stored in variable *SUBJECT*.
- PROBIT warns that the data are in a case-by-case form and that the plot is therefore skipped.
- Degrees of freedom for the goodness-of-fit test are based on individual cases, not dosage groups.
- PROBIT displays predicted and observed frequencies for all individual input cases.

Example

```
* Aggregating case-by-case data

DATA LIST FREE/PREPARTN DOSE RESPONSE.
BEGIN DATA
     1.00     1.50        .00
     ...
     4.00    20.00       1.00
END DATA.
AGGREGATE OUTFILE=*
  /BREAK=PREPARTN DOSE
  /SUBJECTS=N(RESPONSE)
  /NRESP=SUM(RESPONSE).
PROBIT NRESP OF SUBJECTS BY PREPARTN(1,4) WITH DOSE.
```

- This example analyzes the same dose-response model as the previous example, but the data are first aggregated.

- AGGREGATE summarizes the data by cases representing all subjects who received the same preparation (*PREPARTN*) at the same dose (*DOSE*).

- The number of cases having a nonmissing response is recorded in the aggregated variable *SUBJECTS*.

- Because *RESPONSE* is coded 0 for no response and 1 for a response, the sum of the values gives the number of observations with a response.

- PROBIT requests a default analysis.

- The parameter estimates for this analysis are the same as those calculated for individual cases in the example above. The chi-square test, however, is based on the number of dosages.

Variable Specification

The variable specification on PROBIT identifies the variables for response count, observation count, groups, and predictors. The variable specification is required.

- The variables must be specified first. The specification must include the response-count variable, followed by the keyword OF and then the observation-count variable.

- If the value of the response-count variable exceeds that of the observation-count variable, a procedure error occurs and PROBIT is not executed.

- At least one predictor (covariate) must be specified following the keyword WITH. The number of predictors is limited only by available workspace. All predictors must be continuous variables.

- You can specify a grouping variable (factor) after the keyword BY. Only one variable can be specified. It must be numeric and can contain only integer values. You must specify, in parentheses, a range indicating the minimum and maximum values for the grouping variable. Each integer value in the specified range defines a group.

- Cases with values for the grouping variable that are outside the specified range are excluded from the analysis.

- Keywords BY and WITH can appear in either order. However, both must follow the response- and observation-count variables.

Example

```
PROBIT R OF N WITH X.
```

- The number of observations having the measured response appears in variable *R*, and the total number of observations is in *N*. The predictor is *X*.

Example

```
PROBIT  R OF N BY ROOT(1,2) WITH X.

PROBIT  R OF N WITH X BY ROOT(1,2).
```

- Because keywords BY and WITH can be used in either order, these two commands are equivalent. Each command specifies *X* as a continuous predictor and *ROOT* as a categorical grouping variable.
- Groups are identified by the levels of variable *ROOT*, which may be 1 or 2.
- For each combination of predictor and grouping variables, the variable *R* contains the number of observations with the response of interest, and *N* contains the total number of observations.

MODEL Subcommand

MODEL specifies the form of the dichotomous-response model. Response models can be thought of as transformations (*T*) of response rates, which are proportions or probabilities (*p*). Note the difference in the transformations between the current version and the previous versions.

- A **probit** is the inverse of the cumulative standard normal distribution function. Thus, for any proportion, the probit transformation returns the value below which that proportion of standard normal deviates is found. For the probit response model, the program uses $T(p) = \text{PROBIT}(p)$. Hence:

$$T(0.025) = \text{PROBIT}(0.025) = -1.96$$
$$T(0.400) = \text{PROBIT}(0.400) = -0.25$$
$$T(0.500) = \text{PROBIT}(0.500) = 0.00$$
$$T(0.950) = \text{PROBIT}(0.950) = 1.64$$

- A **logit** is simply the natural log of the odds ratio, $p/(1-p)$. In the Probit procedure, the response function is given as $T(p) = \log_e(p/(1-p))$. Hence:

$$T(0.025) = \text{LOGIT}(0.025) = -3.66$$
$$T(0.400) = \text{LOGIT}(0.400) = -0.40$$
$$T(0.500) = \text{LOGIT}(0.500) = 0.00$$
$$T(0.950) = \text{LOGIT}(0.950) = 2.94$$

You can request one or both of the models on the MODEL subcommand. The default is PROBIT if the subcommand is not specified or is specified with no keyword.

PROBIT *Probit response model.* This is the default.

LOGIT *Logit response model.*

BOTH *Both probit and logit response models.* PROBIT displays all the output for the logit model followed by the output for the probit model.

- If subgroups and multiple-predictor variables are defined, PROBIT estimates a separate intercept, a_j, for each subgroup and a regression coefficient, b_i, for each predictor.

LOG Subcommand

LOG specifies the base of the logarithmic transformation of the predictor variables or suppresses the default log transformation.

- LOG applies to all predictors.
- To transform only selected predictors, use COMPUTE commands before the Probit procedure. Then specify NONE on the LOG subcommand.
- If LOG is omitted, a logarithm base of 10 is used.
- If LOG is used without a specification, the natural logarithm base e (2.718) is used.
- If you have a control group in your data and specify NONE on the LOG subcommand, the control group is included in the analysis. See the NATRES subcommand on p. 166.

You can specify one of the following on LOG:

value *Logarithm base to be applied to all predictors.*

NONE *No transformation of the predictors.*

Example

```
PROBIT R OF N BY ROOT (1,2) WITH X
  /LOG = 2.
```

- LOG specifies a base-2 logarithmic transformation.

CRITERIA Subcommand

Use CRITERIA to specify the values of control parameters for the PROBIT algorithm. You can specify any or all of the keywords below. Defaults remain in effect for parameters that are not changed.

OPTOL(n) *Optimality tolerance.* Alias CONVERGE. If an iteration point is a feasible point and the next step will not produce a relative change in either the parameter vector or the log-likelihood function of more than the square root of n, an optimal solution has been found. OPTOL can also be thought of as the number of significant digits in the log-likelihood function at the solution. For example, if OPTOL=10^{-6}, the log-likelihood function should have approximately six significant digits of accuracy. The default value is machine epsilon**0.8.

ITERATE(n)   *Iteration limit.* Specify the maximum number of iterations. The default is $\max(50, 3(p + 1))$, where p is the number of parameters in the model.

P(p)   *Heterogeneity criterion probability.* Specify a cutoff value between 0 and 1 for the significance of the goodness-of-fit test. The cutoff value determines whether a heterogeneity factor is included in calculations of confidence levels for effective levels of a predictor. If the significance of chi-square is greater than the cutoff, the heterogeneity factor is not included. If you specify 0, this criterion is disabled; if you specify 1, a heterogeneity factor is automatically included. The default is 0.15.

STEPLIMIT(n)   *Step limit.* The PROBIT algorithm does not allow changes in the length of the parameter vector to exceed a factor of n. This limit prevents very early steps from going too far from good initial estimates. Specify any positive value. The default value is 0.1.

CONVERGE(n)   *Alias of OPTOL.*

NATRES Subcommand

You can use NATRES either to supply a known natural response rate to be used in the solution or to instruct PROBIT to estimate the natural (or threshold) response rate of the model.

- To supply a known natural response rate as a constraint on the model solution, specify a value less than 1 on NATRES.

- To instruct PROBIT to estimate the natural response rate of the model, you can indicate a control group by giving a 0 value to any of the predictor variables. PROBIT displays the estimate of the natural response rate and the standard error and includes the estimate in the covariance/correlation matrix as NAT RESP.

- If no control group is indicated and NATRES is specified without a given value, PROBIT estimates the natural response rate from the entire data and informs you that no control group has been provided. The estimate of the natural response rate and the standard error are displayed and NAT RESP is included in the covariance/correlation matrix.

- If you have a control group in your data and specify NONE on the LOG subcommand, the control group is included in the analysis.

Example

```
DATA LIST FREE / SOLUTION DOSE NOBSN NRESP.
BEGIN DATA
1   5 100 20
1  10  80 30
1   0 100 10
...
END DATA.

PROBIT NRESP OF NOBSN BY SOLUTION(1,4) WITH DOSE
  /NATRES.
```

- This example reads four variables and requests a default analysis with an estimate of the natural response rate.
- The predictor variable, *DOSE*, has a value of 0 for the third case.
- The response count (10) and the observation count (100) for this case establish the initial estimate of the natural response rate.
- Because the default log transformation is performed, the control group is not included in the analysis.

Example

```
DATA LIST FREE / SOLUTION DOSE NOBSN NRESP.
BEGIN DATA
1   5 100 20
1 10   80 30
1   0 100 10
  ...
END DATA.

PROBIT NRESP OF NOBSN BY SOLUTION(1,4) WITH DOSE
  /NATRES = 0.10.
```

- This example reads four variables and requests an analysis in which the natural response rate is set to 0.10. The values of the control group are ignored.
- The control group is excluded from the analysis because the default log transformation is performed.

PRINT Subcommand

Use PRINT to control the statistics calculated by PROBIT.

- PROBIT always displays the plot (for a single-predictor model) and the parameter estimates and covariances for the probit model.
- If PRINT is used, the requested statistics are calculated and displayed in addition to the parameter estimates and plot.
- If PRINT is not specified or is specified without any keyword, FREQ, CI, and RMP are calculated and displayed in addition to the parameter estimates and plot.

DEFAULT   *FREQ, CI, and RMP*. This is the default if PRINT is not specified or is specified by itself.

FREQ   *Frequencies*. Display a table of observed and predicted frequencies with their residual values. If observations are entered on a case-by-case basis, this listing can be quite lengthy.

CI   *Fiducial confidence intervals*. Print Finney's (1971) fiducial confidence intervals for the levels of the predictor needed to produce each proportion of responses. PROBIT displays this default output for single-predictor models only. If a categorical grouping variable is specified, PROBIT produces a table of confidence intervals for each group. If the Pearson chi-square goodness-of-fit test is significant ($p < 0.15$ by default), PROBIT uses a heterogeneity factor to calculate the limits.

RMP   *Relative median potency.* Display the relative median potency (RMP) of each pair of groups defined by the grouping variable. PROBIT displays this default output for single-predictor models only. For any pair of groups, the RMP is the ratio of the stimulus tolerances in those groups. **Stimulus tolerance** is the value of the predictor necessary to produce a 50% response rate. If the derived model for one predictor and two groups estimates that a predictor value of 21 produces a 50% response rate in the first group, and that a predictor value of 15 produces a 50% response rate in the second group, the relative median potency would be 21/15 = 1.40. In biological assay analyses, RMP measures the comparative strength of preparations.

PARALL   *Parallelism test.* Produce a test of the parallelism of regression lines for different levels of the grouping variable. This test displays a chi-square value and its associated probability. It requires an additional pass through the data and, thus, additional processing time.

NONE   *Display only the unconditional output.* This option can be used to override any other specification on the PRINT subcommand for PROBIT.

ALL   *All available output.* This is the same as requesting FREQ, CI, RMP, and PARALL.

MISSING Subcommand

PROBIT always deletes cases having a missing value for any variable. In the output, PROBIT indicates how many cases it rejected because of missing data. This information is displayed with the DATA Information that prints at the beginning of the output. You can use the MISSING subcommand to control the treatment of user-missing values.

EXCLUDE   *Delete cases with user-missing values.* This is the default. You can also make it explicit by using the keyword DEFAULT.

INCLUDE   *Include user-missing values.* PROBIT treats user-missing values as valid. Only cases with system-missing values are rejected.

2SLS

```
2SLS [EQUATION=]dependent variable WITH predictor variable

[/[EQUATION=]dependent variable...]

 /INSTRUMENTS=varlist

[/ENDOGENOUS=varlist]

[/{CONSTANT**}
  {NOCONSTANT}

[/PRINT=COV]

[/SAVE = [PRED] [RESID]]

[/APPLY[='model name']]
```

**Default if the subcommand or keyword is omitted.

Example:

```
2SLS VAR01 WITH VAR02 VAR03
  /INSTRUMENTS VAR03 LAGVAR01.
```

Overview

2SLS performs two-stage least-squares regression to produce consistent estimates of param-eters when one or more predictor variables might be correlated with the disturbance. This sit-uation typically occurs when your model consists of a system of simultaneous equations wherein endogenous variables are specified as predictors in one or more of the equations. The two-stage least-squares technique uses instrumental variables to produce regressors that are not contemporaneously correlated with the disturbance. Parameters of a single equation or a set of simultaneous equations can be estimated.

Options

New Variables. You can change NEWVAR settings on the TSET command prior to 2SLS to eval-uate the regression statistics without saving the values of predicted and residual variables, or save the new values to replace the values saved earlier, or save the new values without erasing values saved earlier (see the TSET command in the *SPSS Base Syntax Reference Guide*). You can also use the SAVE subcommand on 2SLS to override the NONE or the default CURRENT settings on NEWVAR.

Covariance Matrix. You can obtain the covariance matrix of the parameter estimates in addition to all of the other output by specifying PRINT=DETAILED on the TSET command prior to 2SLS. You can also use the PRINT subcommand to obtain the covariance matrix regardless of the setting on PRINT.

Basic Specification

The basic specification is at least one EQUATION subcommand and one INSTRUMENTS subcommand.

- For each equation specified, 2SLS estimates and displays the regression analysis-of-variance table, regression standard error, mean of the residuals, parameter estimates, standard errors of the parameter estimates, standardized parameter estimates, t statistic significance tests and probability levels for the parameter estimates, tolerance of the variables, the parameter estimates, and correlation matrix of the parameter estimates.
- If the setting on NEWVAR is either ALL or the default CURRENT, two new variables containing the predicted and residual values are automatically created for each equation. The variables are labeled and added to the working data file.

Subcommand Order

- Subcommands can be specified in any order.

Syntax Rules

- The INSTRUMENTS subcommand must specify at least as many variables as are specified after WITH on the longest EQUATION subcommand.
- If a subcommand is specified more than once, the effect is cumulative (except for the APPLY subcommand, which executes only the last occurrence).

Operations

- 2SLS cannot produce forecasts beyond the length of any regressor series.
- 2SLS honors the SPSS WEIGHT command.
- 2SLS uses listwise deletion of missing data. Whenever a variable is missing a value for a particular observation, that observation will not be used in any of the computations.

EQUATION Subcommand

EQUATION specifies the structural equations for the model and is required. The actual keyword EQUATION is optional.

- An equation specifies a single dependent variable, followed by keyword WITH and one or more predictor variables.
- You can specify more than one equation. Multiple equations are separated by slashes.

Example

```
2SLS EQUATION=Y1 WITH X1 X2
  /INSTRUMENTS=X1 LAGX2 X3.
```

- In this example, *Y1* is the dependent variable and *X1* and *X2* are the predictors. The instruments used to predict the *X2* values are *X1*, *LAGX2*, and *X3*.

INSTRUMENTS Subcommand

INSTRUMENTS specifies the instrumental variables. These variables are used to compute predicted values for the endogenous variables in the first stage of 2SLS.

- At least one INSTRUMENTS subcommand must be specified.
- If more than one INSTRUMENTS subcommand is specified, the effect is cumulative. All variables named on INSTRUMENTS subcommands are used as instruments to predict all the endogenous variables.
- Any variable in the working data file can be named as an instrument.
- Instrumental variables can be specified on the EQUATION subcommand, but this is not required.
- The INSTRUMENTS subcommand must name at least as many variables as are specified after WITH on the longest EQUATION subcommand.
- If all the predictor variables are listed as the only INSTRUMENTS, the results are the same as results from ordinary least-squares regression.

Example

```
2SLS DEMAND WITH PRICE, INCOME
 /PRICE WITH DEMAND, RAINFALL, LAGPRICE
 /INSTRUMENTS=INCOME, RAINFALL, LAGPRICE.
```

- The endogenous variables are PRICE and DEMAND.
- The instruments to be used to compute predicted values for the endogenous variables are INCOME, RAINFALL, and LAGPRICE.

ENDOGENOUS Subcommand

All variables not specified on the INSTRUMENTS subcommand are used as endogenous variables by 2SLS. The ENDOGENOUS subcommand simply allows you to document what these variables are.

- Computations are not affected by specifications on the ENDOGENOUS subcommand.

Example

```
2SLS Y1 WITH X1 X2 X3
 /INSTRUMENTS=X2 X4 LAGY1
 /ENDOGENOUS=Y1 X1 X3.
```

- In this example, the ENDOGENOUS subcommand is specified to document the endogenous variables.

CONSTANT and NOCONSTANT Subcommands

Specify CONSTANT or NOCONSTANT to indicate whether a constant term should be estimated in the regression equation. The specification of either subcommand overrides the CONSTANT setting on the TSET command for the current procedure.

- CONSTANT is the default and specifies that the constant term is used as an instrument.
- NOCONSTANT eliminates the constant term.

SAVE Subcommand

SAVE saves the values of predicted and residual variables generated during the current session to the end of the working data file. The default names *FIT_n* and *ERR_n* will be generated, where *n* increments each time variables are saved for an equation. SAVE overrides the NONE or the default CURRENT setting on NEWVAR for the current procedure.

PRED   *Save the predicted value.* The new variable is named *FIT_n*, where *n* increments each time a predicted or residual variable is saved for an equation.

RESSID   *Save the residual value.* The new variable is named *ERR_n*, where *n* increments each time a predicted or residual variable is saved for an equation.

PRINT Subcommand

PRINT can be used to produce an additional covariance matrix for each equation. The only specification on this subcommand is keyword COV. The PRINT subcommand overrides the PRINT setting on the TSET command for the current procedure.

APPLY Subcommand

APPLY allows you to use a previously defined 2SLS model without having to repeat the specifications.

- The only specification on APPLY is the name of a previous model. If a model name is not specified, the model specified on the previous 2SLS command is used.
- To change the series used with the model, enter new series names before or after the APPLY subcommand.
- To change one or more model specifications, specify the subcommands of only those portions you want to change after the APPLY subcommand.
- If no series are specified on the command, the series that were originally specified with the model being reapplied are used.

Example

```
2SLS Y1 WITH X1 X2 / X1 WITH Y1 X2
  /INSTRUMENTS=X2 X3.
2SLS APPLY
  /INSTRUMENTS=X2 X3 LAGX1.
```

- In this example, the first command requests 2SLS using *X2* and *X3* as instruments.
- The second command specifies the same equations but changes the instruments to *X2*, *X3*, and *LAGX1*.

WLS

```
WLS [VARIABLES=]dependent varname WITH independent varnames

[/SOURCE=varname]

[/DELTA=[{1.0**                    }]]
          {value list             }
          {value TO value BY value}

[/WEIGHT=varname]

[/{CONSTANT**}
  {NOCONSTANT}

[/PRINT={BEST}]
        {ALL }

[/SAVE = WEIGHT]

[/APPLY[='model name']]
```

**Default if the subcommand or keyword is omitted.

Example:

```
WLS VARY WITH VARX VARZ
  /SOURCE=VARZ
  /DELTA=2.
```

Overview

WLS (weighted least squares) estimates regression models with different weights for different cases. Weighted least squares should be used when errors from an ordinary regression are heteroscedastic—that is, when the size of the residual is a function of the magnitude of some variable, termed the **source**.

The WLS model is a simple regression model in which the residual variance is a function of the source variable, up to some power transform indicated by a delta value. For fuller regression results, save the weights produced by WLS and specify that weight variable on the REGWGT subcommand in REGRESSION.

Options

Calculated and Specified Weights. WLS can calculate the weights based on a source variable and delta values (subcommands SOURCE and DELTA), or it can apply existing weights contained in a series (subcommand WEIGHT). If weights are calculated, each weight value is calculated as the source series value raised to the negative delta value.

New Variables. You can change NEWVAR settings on the TSET command prior to WLS to evaluate the regression coefficients and log-likelihood function without saving the weight variable, or save the new values to replace the values saved earlier, or save the new values without erasing values saved earlier (see the TSET command in the *SPSS Base Syntax Reference Guide*). You can also use the SAVE subcommand on WLS to override the NONE or the default CURRENT settings on NEWVAR for the current procedure.

Statistical Output. You can change the PRINT setting on the TSET command prior to WLS to display regression coefficients or the list of log-likelihood functions at each delta value, or to limit the output to only the regression statistics for the delta value at which the log-likelihood function is maximized (see the TSET command in the *SPSS Base Syntax Reference Guide*). You can also use the PRINT subcommand to override the PRINT setting on the TSET command for the current procedure and obtain regression coefficients at each value of delta in addition to the default output.

Basic Specification

- The basic specification is the VARIABLES subcommand specifying one dependent variable, the keyword WITH, and one or more independent variables. Weights are calculated using the first independent variable as the source variable and a default delta value of 1.
- The default output for calculated weights displays the log-likelihood function for each value of delta. For the value of delta at which the log-likelihood function is maximized, the displayed summary regression statistics include R, R^2, adjusted R^2, standard errors, analysis of variance, and t tests of the individual coefficients. A variable named *WGT#1* containing the calculated weights is automatically created, labeled, and added to the working data file.

Syntax Rules

- VARIABLES can be specified only once.
- DELTA can be specified more than once. Each specification will be executed.
- If other subcommands are specified more than once, only the last specification of each one is executed.
- You can specify either SOURCE and DELTA, or just the WEIGHT subcommand. You cannot specify all three, and you cannot specify WEIGHT with SOURCE or with DELTA.

Subcommand Order

- Subcommands can be specified in any order.

Operations

- If neither the WEIGHT subcommand nor the SOURCE and DELTA subcommands are specified, a warning is issued and weights are calculated using the default source and delta value.
- Only one *WGT#1* variable is created per procedure. If more than one delta value is specified, the weights used when the log-likelihood function is maximized are the ones saved as *WGT#1*.
- *WGT#1* is not created when the WEIGHT subcommand is used.

- The SPSS WEIGHT command specifies case replication weights, which are *not* the same as the weights used in weighted least squares. If the WEIGHT command and WLS WEIGHT subcommand are both specified, both types of weights are incorporated in WLS.
- WLS uses listwise deletion of missing values. Whenever one variable is missing a value for a particular observation, that observation will not be included in any computations.

Limitations

- Maximum one VARIABLES subcommand.
- Maximum one dependent variable on the VARIABLES subcommand. There is no limit on the number of independent variables.
- Maximum 150 values specified on the DELTA subcommand.

Example

```
WLS VARY WITH VARX VARZ
  /SOURCE=VARZ
  /DELTA=2.
```

- This command specifies a weighted least-squares regression in which *VARY* is the dependent variable and *VARX* and *VARZ* are the independent variables.
- *VARZ* is identified as the source of heteroscedasticity.
- Weights will be calculated using a delta value of 2. Thus, the weights will equal $VARZ^{-2}$.

VARIABLES Subcommand

VARIABLES specifies the variable list and is the only required subcommand. The actual keyword VARIABLES can be omitted.

SOURCE Subcommand

SOURCE is used in conjunction with the DELTA subcommand to compute weights. SOURCE names the variable that is the source of heteroscedasticity.

- The only specification on SOURCE is the name of a variable to be used as the source of heteroscedasticity.
- Only one source variable can be specified.
- If neither SOURCE nor WEIGHT is specified, the first independent variable specified on the VARIABLES subcommand is assumed to be the source variable.

DELTA Subcommand

DELTA, alias POWER, is used in conjunction with the SOURCE subcommand to compute weights. DELTA specifies the values to use in computing weights. The weights are equal to 1/(SOURCE raised to the DELTA power).

- The specification on DELTA is a list of possible delta values and/or value grids.
- Multiple values and grids can be specified on one DELTA subcommand.
- Delta values can be any value in the range of –6.5 to +7.5. Values below this range are assigned the minimum (–6.5), and values above are assigned the maximum (7.5).
- A grid is specified by naming the starting value, the keyword TO, an ending value, the keyword BY, and an increment value. Alternatively, the keyword BY and the increment value can be specified after the starting value.
- More than one DELTA subcommand can be specified; each subcommand will be executed.
- If DELTA is not specified, the delta value defaults to 1.0.

Example

```
WLS X1 WITH Y1 Z1
  /SOURCE=Z1
  /DELTA=0.5.
```

- In this example, weights are calculated using the source variable *Z1* and a delta value of 0.5. Thus, the weights are 1/(SQRT (Z1)).

Example

```
WLS SHARES WITH PRICE
  /DELTA=0.5 TO 2.5 BY 0.5.
```

- In this example, several regression equations will be fit, one for each value of delta.
- Weights are calculated using the source variable *PRICE* (the default).
- The delta values start at 0.5 and go up to 2.5, incrementing by 0.5. This specification is equivalent to 0.5 BY 0.5 TO 2.5.
- The weights that maximize the log-likelihood function will be saved as variable *WGT#1*.

WEIGHT Subcommand

WEIGHT specifies the variable containing the weights to be used in weighting the cases. WEIGHT is an alternative to computing the weights using the SOURCE and DELTA subcommands. If a variable containing weights is specified, the output includes the regression coefficients, log-likelihood function, and summary regression statistics such as R, R^2, adjusted R^2, standard errors, analysis of variance, and t tests of the coefficients. Since no new weights are computed, no new variable is created. For a description of the output when weights are calculated by WLS, see "Basic Specification" on p. 174.

- The only specification on WEIGHT is the name of the variable containing the weights. Typically, *WGT* variables from previous WLS procedures are used.
- Only one variable can be specified.

Example

```
WLS SHARES WITH PRICE
  /WEIGHT=WGT_1.
```

- This WLS command uses the weights contained in variable *WGT_1* to weight cases.

CONSTANT and NOCONSTANT Subcommands

Specify CONSTANT or NOCONSTANT to indicate whether a constant term should be estimated in the regression equation. The specification of either subcommand overrides the CONSTANT setting on the TSET command for the current procedure.

- CONSTANT is the default and specifies that the constant term is used as an instrument.
- NOCONSTANT eliminates the constant term.

SAVE Subcommand

SAVE saves the weight variable generated during the current session to the end of the working data file. The default name *WGT_n* will be generated, where *n* increments to make the variable name unique. The only specification on SAVE is WEIGHT. The specification overrides the NONE or the default CURRENT setting on NEWVAR for the current procedure.

PRINT Subcommand

PRINT can be used to override the PRINT setting on the TSET command for the current procedure. Two keywords are available.

BEST   *Display coefficients for the best weight only.* This is the default.

ALL   *Display coefficients for all weights.*

APPLY Subcommand

- The APPLY subcommand allows you to use a previously defined WLS model without having to repeat the specifications.
- The only specification on APPLY is the name of a previous model in quotes. If a model name is not specified, the model specified on the previous WLS command is used.
- To change one or more model specifications, specify the subcommands of only those portions you want to change after the APPLY subcommand.
- If no variables are specified on the command, the variables that were originally specified with the model being reapplied arc uscd.

Example

```
WLS X1 WITH Y1
  /SOURCE=Y1
  /DELTA=1.5.
WLS APPLY
  /DELTA=2.
```

- The first command produces a weighted least-squares regression of *X1*, with *Y1* as the source variable and delta equal to 1.5.
- The second command uses the same variable and source but changes the delta value to 2.

Example

```
WLS X1 WITH Y1 Z1
  /SOURCE=Z1
  /DELTA=1 TO 3 BY 0.5
WLS APPLY
  /WEIGHT=WGT#1.
```

- The first command regresses *X1* on *Y1* and *Z1*, using *Z1* as the source variable. The delta values range from 1 to 3, incrementing by 0.5.
- The second command again regresses *X1* on *Y1* and *Z1*, but this time applies the values of *WGT#1* as the weights.

Appendix
Categorical Variable
Coding Schemes

In many SPSS procedures, you can request automatic replacement of a categorical independent variable with a set of contrast variables, which will then be entered or removed from an equation as a block. You can specify how the set of contrast variables is to be coded, usually on the CONTRAST subcommand. This appendix explains and illustrates how different contrast types requested on CONTRAST actually work.

Deviation

Deviation from the grand mean. In matrix terms, these contrasts have the form:

```
mean      (   1/k      1/k      ...      1/k      1/k )
df(1)     ( 1-1/k     -1/k      ...     -1/k     -1/k )
df(2)     (  -1/k    1-1/k      ...     -1/k     -1/k )
  .                     .
  .                     .

df(k-1)   (  -1/k     -1/k      ...    1-1/k     -1/k )
```

where k is the number of categories for the independent variable and the last category is omitted by default. For example, the deviation contrasts for an independent variable with three categories are as follows:

```
(  1/3      1/3      1/3 )
(  2/3     -1/3     -1/3 )
( -1/3      2/3     -1/3 )
```

To omit a category other than the last, specify the number of the omitted category in parentheses after the DEVIATION keyword. For example, the following subcommand obtains the deviations for the first and third categories and omits the second:

```
/CONTRAST(FACTOR)=DEVIATION(2)
```

Suppose that *factor* has three categories. The resulting contrast matrix will be

```
(   1/3        1/3       1/3 )
(   2/3       -1/3      -1/3 )
(  -1/3       -1/3       2/3 )
```

Simple

Simple contrasts. Compares each level of a factor to the last. The general matrix form is

```
mean   (  1/k       1/k        ...      1/k     1/k )
df(1)  (   1         0         ...       0      -1 )
df(2)  (   0         1         ...       0      -1 )
  .                    .
  .                    .
df(k-1) (   0         0         ...       1      -1 )
```

where k is the number of categories for the independent variable. For example, the simple contrasts for an independent variable with four categories are as follows:

```
( 1/4       1/4       1/4       1/4 )
(  1         0         0        -1 )
(  0         1         0        -1 )
(  0         0         1        -1 )
```

To use another category instead of the last as a reference category, specify in parentheses after the SIMPLE keyword the sequence number of the reference category, which is not necessarily the value associated with that category. For example, the following CONTRAST subcommand obtains a contrast matrix that omits the second category:

```
/CONTRAST(FACTOR) = SIMPLE(2)
```

Suppose that *factor* has four categories. The resulting contrast matrix will be

```
( 1/4       1/4       1/4       1/4 )
(  1        -1         0         0 )
(  0        -1         1         0 )
(  0        -1         0         1 )
```

Helmert

Helmert contrasts. Compares categories of an independent variable with the mean of the subsequent categories. The general matrix form is

mean	($1/k$	$1/k$	...	$1/k$	$1/k$)
df(1)	(1	$-1/(k-1)$	...	$-1/(k-1)$	$-1/(k-1)$)
df(2)	(0	1	...	$-1/(k-2)$	$-1/(k-2)$)
.		.			
.		.			
.		.			
df(k-2)	(0	0	1	-1/2	-1/2)
df(k-1)	(0	0	...	1	-1)

where k is the number of categories of the independent variable. For example, an independent variable with four categories has a Helmert contrast matrix of the following form:

(1/4	1/4	1/4	1/4)
(1	-1/3	-1/3	-1/3)
(0	1	-1/2	-1/2)
(0	0	1	-1)

Difference

Difference or reverse Helmert contrasts. Compares categories of an independent variable with the mean of the previous categories of the variable. The general matrix form is

mean	($1/k$	$1/k$	$1/k$	...	$1/k$)
df(1)	(-1	1	0	...	0)
df(2)	(-1/2	-1/2	1	...	0)
.		.			
.		.			
df(k-1)	($-1/(k-1)$	$-1/(k-1)$	$-1/(k-1)$	...	1)

where k is the number of categories for the independent variable. For example, the difference contrasts for an independent variable with four categories are as follows:

(1/4	1/4	1/4	1/4)
(-1	1	0	0)
(-1/2	-1/2	1	0)
(-1/3	-1/3	-1/3	1)

Polynomial

Orthogonal polynomial contrasts. The first degree of freedom contains the linear effect across all categories; the second degree of freedom, the quadratic effect; the third degree of freedom, the cubic; and so on for the higher-order effects.

You can specify the spacing between levels of the treatment measured by the given categorical variable. Equal spacing, which is the default if you omit the metric, can be specified as consecutive integers from 1 to k, where k is the number of categories. If the variable *drug* has three categories, the subcommand

```
/CONTRAST(DRUG)=POLYNOMIAL
```

is the same as

```
/CONTRAST(DRUG)=POLYNOMIAL(1,2,3)
```

Equal spacing is not always necessary, however. For example, suppose that *drug* represents different dosages of a drug given to three groups. If the dosage administered to the second group is twice that to the first group and the dosage administered to the third group is three times that to the first group, the treatment categories are equally spaced, and an appropriate metric for this situation consists of consecutive integers:

```
/CONTRAST(DRUG)=POLYNOMIAL(1,2,3)
```

If, however, the dosage administered to the second group is four times that given the first group, and the dosage given the third group is seven times that to the first, an appropriate metric is

```
/CONTRAST(DRUG)=POLYNOMIAL(1,4,7)
```

In either case, the result of the contrast specification is that the first degree of freedom for *drug* contains the linear effect of the dosage levels and the second degree of freedom contains the quadratic effect.

Polynomial contrasts are especially useful in tests of trends and for investigating the nature of response surfaces. You can also use polynomial contrasts to perform nonlinear curve fitting, such as curvilinear regression.

Repeated

Compares adjacent levels of an independent variable. The general matrix form is

mean	($1/k$	$1/k$	$1/k$	...	$1/k$	$1/k$)
df(1)	(1	-1	0	...	0	0)
df(2)	(0	1	-1	...	0	0)
.		.				
.		.				
df(k-1)	(0	0	0	...	1	-1)

where k is the number of categories for the independent variable. For example, the repeated contrasts for an independent variable with four categories are as follows:

```
( 1/4      1/4      1/4      1/4 )
(  1       -1        0        0 )
(  0        1       -1        0 )
(  0        0        1       -1 )
```

These contrasts are useful in profile analysis and wherever difference scores are needed.

Special

A user-defined contrast. Allows entry of special contrasts in the form of square matrices with as many rows and columns as there are categories of the given independent variable. For MANOVA and LOGLINEAR, the first row entered is always the mean, or constant, effect and represents the set of weights indicating how to average other independent variables, if any, over the given variable. Generally, this contrast is a vector of ones.

The remaining rows of the matrix contain the special contrasts indicating the desired comparisons between categories of the variable. Usually, orthogonal contrasts are the most useful. Orthogonal contrasts are statistically independent and are nonredundant. Contrasts are orthogonal if:

- For each row, contrast coefficients sum to zero.

- The products of corresponding coefficients for all pairs of disjoint rows also sum to zero.

For example, suppose that *treatment* has four levels and that you want to compare the various levels of treatment with each other. An appropriate special contrast is

```
(  1    1    1    1 )    weights for mean calculation
(  3   -1   -1   -1 )    compare 1st with 2nd through 4th
(  0    2   -1   -1 )    compare 2nd with 3rd and 4th
(  0    0    1   -1 )    compare 3rd with 4th
```

which you specify by means of the following CONTRAST subcommand for MANOVA, LOGISTIC REGRESSION, and COXREG:

```
/CONTRAST(TREATMNT)=SPECIAL( 1  1  1  1
                             3 -1 -1 -1
                             0  2 -1 -1
                             0  0  1 -1 )
```

For LOGLINEAR, you need to specify:

```
/CONTRAST(TREATMNT)=BASIS SPECIAL( 1  1  1  1
                                   3 -1 -1 -1
                                   0  2 -1 -1
                                   0  0  1 -1 )
```

Each row except the means row sums to zero. Products of each pair of disjoint rows sum to zero as well:

Rows 2 and 3: $(3)(0) + (-1)(2) + (-1)(-1) + (-1)(-1) = 0$

Rows 2 and 4: $(3)(0) + (-1)(0) + (-1)(1) + (-1)(-1) = 0$

Rows 3 and 4: $(0)(0) + (2)(0) + (-1)(1) + (-1)(-1) = 0$

The special contrasts need not be orthogonal. However, they must not be linear combinations of each other. If they are, the procedure reports the linear dependency and ceases processing. Helmert, difference, and polynomial contrasts are all orthogonal contrasts.

Indicator

Indicator variable coding. Also known as dummy coding, this is not available in LOGLINEAR or MANOVA. The number of new variables coded is $k - 1$. Cases in the reference category are coded 0 for all $k - 1$ variables. A case in the ith category is coded 0 for all indicator variables except the ith, which is coded 1.

Bibliography

Agresti, A. 1990. *Categorical data analysis*. New York: John Wiley and Sons.

Aldrich, J. H., and F. D. Nelson. 1984. *Linear probability, logit, and probit models*. Beverly Hills, Calif.: Sage Publications.

Andrews, D. F., R. Gnanadesikan, and J. L. Warner. 1973. Methods for assessing multivariate normality. In: *Multivariate Analysis III*, P. R. Krishnaiah, ed. New York: Academic Press.

Atkinson, A. C. 1980. A note on the generalized information criterion for choice of a model. *Biometrika*, 67: 413–418.

Berry, W. D. 1984. *Nonrecursive causal models*. Beverly Hills, Calif.: Sage Publications.

Brown, B. W., Jr. 1980. Prediction analyses for binary data. In: *Biostatistics Casebook*, R. G. Miller, B. Efron, B. W. Brown, and L. E. Moses, eds. New York: John Wiley and Sons.

Carroll, J. D., and J. J. Chang. 1970. Analysis of individual differences in multidimensional scaling via an *n*-way generalization of "Eckart-Young" decomposition. *Psychometrika*, 35: 238–319.

Churchill, G. A., Jr. 1979. *Marketing research: Methodological foundations*. Hinsdale, Ill.: Dryden Press.

Consumer Reports. 1983. Beer. *Consumer Reports*, July, 342–348.

Draper, N. R., and H. Smith. 1981. *Applied regression analysis*. New York: John Wiley and Sons.

Finn, J. D. 1974. *A general model for multivariate analysis*. New York: Holt, Rinehart and Winston.

Finney, D. J. 1971. *Probit analysis*. Cambridge: Cambridge University Press.

Fox, J. 1984. *Linear statistical models and related methods: With applications to social research*. New York: John Wiley and Sons.

Gilbert, E. S. 1968. On discrimination using qualitative variables. *Journal of the American Statistical Association*, 63: 1399–1412.

Gill, P. E., W. M. Murray, and M. H. Wright. 1981. *Practical optimization*. London: Academic Press.

Gill, P. E., W. M. Murray, M. A. Saunders, and M. H. Wright. 1986. User's guide for NPSOL (version 4.0): A FORTRAN package for nonlinear programming. *Technical Report SOL 86-2*. Department of Operations Research, Stanford University.

Hand, D. J. 1981. *Discrimination and classification*. New York: John Wiley and Sons.

Hanley, J. A., and B. J. McNeil. 1982. The meaning and use of the area under a receiver operating characteristic (ROC) curve. *Radiology*, 143: 29–36.

Hauck, W. W., and A. Donner. 1977. Wald's test as applied to hypotheses in logit analysis. *Journal of the American Statistical Association*, 72: 851–853.

Hosmer, D. W., and S. Lemeshow. 1989. *Applied logistic regression*. New York: John Wiley and Sons.

Jennings, L. S. 1980. Simultaneous equations estimation: Computational aspects. *Journal of Econometrics*, 12: 23–39.

Johnson, R., and D. W. Wichern. 1982. *Applied multivariate statistical analysis*. Englewood Cliffs, N.J.: Prentice-Hall.

Jonassen, C. T., and S. H. Peres. 1960. *Interrelationships of dimensions of community systems*. Columbus: Ohio State University Press.

Kaiser, H. F. 1963. Image analysis. In: *Problems in Measuring Change*, C. W. Harris, ed. Madison: University of Wisconsin Press.

_____. 1970. A second-generation Little Jiffy. *Psychometrika*, 35: 401–415.

Kelejian, H. H., and W. E. Oates. 1989. *Introduction to econometrics: Principles and applications*. 3rd ed. New York: HarperCollins.

Kirk, R. E. 1982. *Experimental design*. 2nd ed. Monterey, Calif.: Brooks/Cole.

Kruskal, J. B. 1964. Nonmetric multidimensional scaling. *Psychometrika*, 29: 1–27, 115–129.

Kshirsager, A. M., and E. Arseven. 1975. A note on the equivalency of two discrimination procedures. *The American Statistician*, 29: 38–39.

Kvalseth, T. O. 1985. Cautionary note about R squared. *The American Statistician*, 39:4, 279–285.

Lawless, J. F., and K. Singhal. 1978. Efficient screening of nonnormal regression models. *Biometrics*, 34: 318–327.

Lord, F. M., and M. R. Novick. 1968. *Statistical theories of mental test scores*. Reading, Mass.: Addison-Wesley.

MacCallum, R. C. 1977. Effects of conditionality on INDSCAL and ALSCAL weights. *Psychometrika*, 42: 297–305.

McCullagh, P., and J. A. Nelder. 1989. *Generalized linear models*. 2nd ed. London: Chapman and Hall.

McGee, V. C. 1968. Multidimensional scaling of n sets of similarity measures: A nonmetric individual differences approach. *Multivariate Behavioral Research*, 3: 233–248.

Milligan, G. W. 1980. An examination of the effect of six types of error perturbation on fifteen clustering algorithms. *Psychometrika*, 45: 325–342.

Moore, D. H. 1973. Evaluation of five discrimination procedures for binary variables. *Journal of the American Statistical Association*, 68: 399.

Morrison, D. F. 1967. *Multivariate statistical methods*. New York: McGraw-Hill.

Nagelkerke, N. J. D. 1991. A note on general definition of the coefficient of determination. *Biometrika*, 78: 691–692.

Nunnally, J. 1978. *Psychometric theory*. 2nd ed. New York: McGraw-Hill.

Rao, C. R. 1973. *Linear statistical inference and its applications*. 2nd ed. New York: John Wiley and Sons.

Simonoff, J. S. 1998. Logistic regression, categorical predictors, and goodness-of-fit: It depends on who you ask. *The American Statistician,* 52: 1: 10–14.

Sneath, P. H. A., and R. R. Sokal. 1973. *Numerical taxonomy*. San Francisco: W. H. Freeman and Co.

Takane, Y., F. W. Young, and J. de Leeuw. 1977. Nonmetric individual differences multidimensional scaling: An alternating least squares method with optimal scaling features. *Psychometrika*, 42: 7–67.

Tatsuoka, M. M. 1971. *Multivariate analysis*. New York: John Wiley and Sons.

Theil, H. 1971. *Principles of econometrics*. New York: John Wiley and Sons.

Torgerson, W. S. 1952. Multidimensional scaling: I. Theory and method. *Psychometrika*, 17: 401–419.

Van Vliet, P. K. J., and J. M. Gupta. 1973. THAM v. sodium bicarbonate in idiopathic respiratory distress syndrome. *Archives of Disease in Childhood*, 48: 249–255.

Young, F. W. 1974. Scaling replicated conditional rank order data. In: *Sociological Methodology*, D. Heise, ed. American Sociological Association, 129–170.

_____. 1975. An asymmetric Euclidean model for multiprocess asymmetric data. In: *Proceedings of US–Japan Seminar on Multidimensional Scaling*.

_____. 1981. Quantitative analysis of qualitative data. *Psychometrika*, 40: 357–387.

Young, F. W., and R. M. Hamer, eds. 1987. *Multidimensional scaling: History, theory, and applications*. Hillsdale, N.J.: Lawrence Erlbaum Associates.

Young, F. W., and R. Lewyckyj. 1979. *ALSCAL–4 user's guide*. Carrboro, N.C.: Data Analysis and Theory Associates.

Simonoff, J. S. 1998. Logistic regression, categorical predictors, and goodness-of-fit: It depends on who you ask. *The American Statistician*, 52, 1: 10–14.

Subject Index

Syntax Index